Personal Finance for Military Families

Pioneer Services Foundation Presents

Personal Finance for Military Families

Foreword by Sergeant Major of the Army Jack L. Tilley, Ret.
Summary by Master Chief Petty Officer of the Navy
Robert J. Walker, Ret.

iUniverse, Inc.
New York Lincoln Shanghai

Pioneer Services Foundation Presents
Personal Finance for Military Families

iUniverse, Inc.

For information address:
iUniverse, Inc.
2021 Pine Lake Road, Suite 100
Lincoln, NE 68512
www.iuniverse.com

ISBN: 0-595-33111-4

Printed in the United States of America

About Pioneer Services Representatives

For over 70 years Pioneer Services Representatives have been helping clients reach their financial goals. Their goal is to help improve operational readiness through education and services that enhance quality of life and financial independence for military families. And since they work exclusively with the military community, they understand the unique financial situation faced by those in the Armed Forces. You can be assured that service members who walk into any Pioneer Services office throughout the country will be treated with the respect and dignity they deserve.

If you would like more information about the services provided by Pioneer Services Representatives, visit www.pioneerservices.com

About the Pioneer Services Foundation

The Pioneer Services Foundation is a non-profit organization created to help the men and women of the Armed Forces become financially educated and to improve their quality of life. The Foundation accomplishes these goals by utilizing the knowledge of retired military personnel and financial experts, and by creating programs and services that assist service members from all ranks and branches.

For more information about the Pioneer Services Foundation, visit their website at www.pioneerservicesfoundation.org.

Acknowledgements

- William D. Sullivan, Pioneer Services Foundation, Director
- Thomas H. Holcom, Pioneer Services Foundation, Director
- Patrick McCarty, Pioneer Services Foundation, Director, West Point Graduate
- Sergeant Major of the Army Jack L. Tilley, Ret., Pioneer Services Foundation, Advisory Board Member
- Master Chief Petty Officer of the Navy Robert J. Walker, Ret., Pioneer Services Foundation, Advisory Board Member
- Jodi Vickery, Military Spouse
- Angie Hollerich, CEP, CCA
- Michael McVey, US Navy

Contents

Foreword

By Sergeant Major of the Army Jack L. Tilley, Ret.

Your Future Starts Today

As the Sergeant Major of the Army, I was an advocate for the men and women in uniform, serving as the Army Chief of Staff's personal advisor on all enlisted-related matters, specifically on training and quality of life issues. Even though I am now retired from my 35 years of duty, I am still focused on helping military families.

Over the years I have seen many financial problems, most of which can be solved by financial education and being able to handle the money situations we face as members of the Armed Forces. I've seen so many young people who don't prepare themselves for the next step in life. They get a little more money and buy too much too soon instead of preparing for the future. Even many NCOs don't know how to define prime, sub-prime and predatory lending. They turn to the wrong resource that they think is going to help them. And they help them all right, with staggering interest rates and long-term, bad debt.

I watched a Soldier when we were in Korea bounce thousands of dollars of checks because he didn't know what was going on with his finances at home. It is difficult to be away from family for periods of time, but it is your responsibility to prepare for those times financially by learning how to keep your checkbook balanced and creating a budget that works for you and your family.

The purpose of this book is to not only help you create a budget and balance your checkbook, but also to give you advice on investing, retirement, and even how to save money on marriage and taxes. This advice will help you for years down the road, including when you leave the service and enter civilian life, whenever that may be. This book offers real-world advice presented in an easy-to-understand way, and can help you make the most of your money.

If I knew 20 or 30 years ago what I know now, I would have made even better choices that would have financially benefited my family earlier and for a longer period of time. I want to help young service members build better lives for their families. And I'm not alone. Your chain of command has experienced leaders that you can tap to your financial advantage. There are also companies out there that truly do care about you, your family, and your financial situation.

As you move on in your career—military or civilian—I suggest that you make the right choices with your finances. It may not always be the easy choice, but the smart move is to limit expenses, increase savings and live within your means.

I hope you enjoy this book, and know that you can take what is written and put it into action. I also thank you for taking the time to care about your finances, and for your service to our great nation.

Sgt. Maj. of the Army Tilley retired in January of 2004 after 35 years of service. He sat on a wide variety of councils and boards that made decisions affecting enlisted Soldiers and their families, and was routinely invited to testify before Congress. He has continued his dedication to service members and their families by serving on the board of the Pioneer Services Foundation.

Chapter One

Budgeting

In the following pages, we will cover these topics:
- Obstacles of Budgeting
- Goals and Purposes of Budgeting
- Benefits of Budgeting
- A Snapshot of Your (Financial) Net Worth: Assets and Liabilities
- How Can You Increase Your Net Worth
- Setting Up Your Budget
- Increasing Your Income vs. Cutting Your Expenses
- Some Budget Hints

A budget is a tool that assists you in managing and controlling your spending and saving. You can use a budget to become more aware of your spending behaviors, to manage your income in a way that maximizes your goals, and to keep an eye on your financial aims. Many people think that budgets are hard work and too complicated to create and adhere to.

They aren't! In reality, if you take just a few minutes out of your schedule each day, working a budget is easy; it's just simple math with a few simple steps.

Obstacles of Budgeting

Don't let the things you hear about budgeting get in the way of your success. You may hear people claiming:
- Budgets are only for people who have lots of money.
- Budgets are only good for people whose money runs out before the month does.
- I have people who will bail me out if I get into financial trouble; I don't need a budget.

1

- I don't have time to budget.
- The longer I'm in the service the more money I'll make, so my problems will go away.
- It's hard to resist all those great deals I see.

There are a number of things wrong with the above statements:

- Budgets are not only for people who have lots of money or for those whose money doesn't run out—budgets are for everyone, even those who seem to be committed to spending more than they make. They are also about establishing a mindset or an attitude about money that says you are not afraid to deal with it often and that you want to be in control of your money instead of having your money control you!
- The comment "I don't have time to budget," is simply not true. Everyone has time; it's simply a matter of how we choose to use that time. Likewise, in relation to spending time dealing with your money, you'll either spend it now to budget and control it or you'll spend it later to clean up your messes with it. It really doesn't take that much time to budget well, especially if you do it on a daily basis. In fact, it may only take 10 to 15 minutes each day. Is that too much time to control your money?
- "The longer I'm in the service the more money I'll make." Let's look at this statement a little more closely. It's true; if you stay in and perform well at your current MOS or Rating, as you meet the time requirements and get promoted—as many of you will—you will earn more money. However, people who earn a lot of money but have poor money management habits also tend to spend more. Moreover, they often spend more than they make. Amazingly, they will even start to think about how they will spend their money, and then, they start to spend it before they even have it!

If you don't manage your money well you'll develop bad money management habits. And it doesn't matter how much a person makes; he or she will still get into money trouble—it will just be bigger money trouble.

Budgeting is the foundation of managing your money and getting into good money habits. Do it now! It's like exercise and a good diet being the foundations of getting in excellent physical shape. It's just like the good study habits, reading, and practice that are the foundations of being good at your MOS or Rating and of being eligible for promotion.

Goals and Purposes of Budgeting

In the budgeting process, you first determine your budget goals, you figure out how much money you have coming into your household, and, most importantly, you find out where your money goes. When you make the decision to have a budget and maintain it, you realize that you will be required to make tough decisions and trade-offs to keep your budget balanced. You will then find that you will be able to improve your budgeting success by learning new spending and saving strategies.

The secrets to money happiness and wealth building are practical and universal. You can learn them and profit from them. When you think of your budget, look at it as a tool to help you manage, control, and evaluate your spending and saving habits.

Do you want to be able to make all of your payments on time so collectors won't hound you? Do you want to be in control of your money instead of allowing it to control you? Do you want to have a car that you can rely upon all of the time yet, at the same time, not be in debt up to your ears? Do you want to have more wealth than your parents, peers, and friends? Do you want to be financially fit someday? If your answer is yes to any of these questions you must start a long-term financial-planning program. It won't happen overnight, but it all starts with budgeting.

Budgeting is simply the process of planning your income so that you can determine how much money is going to come in, how much is going to go out, and where it should go.

The purpose of a budget is to:
- Control your income and your spending;
- Recognize potential (and existing) spending problems;
- Identify how you might overcome such problems; and
- Improve your spending habits.

Your budget balances the various needs of all family members. Most of your budgeting decisions are relatively short-term. A budget also helps you to achieve your long-term goals, such as saving for a car, a home, or your child's college education.

Don't think that by having a budget you will naturally be giving up things you want or that you will have to sacrifice. Think of a budget as a solution, not as a problem. It is the first stepping-stone in the process of getting your finances in order.

The Benefits of Budgeting

Here are a few thoughts concerning the benefits of a budget:

- It helps you to organize your debt and to direct your spending. In turn, you are able to reduce your outstanding debt (past due accounts and loans).
- Pay yourself first! If you put yourself at the top of your budget, it will be the start of both your savings and your investment plan. It's like investing in your military career: If you take a little time on a daily or weekly basis to study for your next promotion, or to hone your skills, you will do better on promotion tests.
- You will pay less in interest and other penalty fees (e.g., bounced check fees and late fees), thereby increasing your spending power. In the end, it will be like increasing your overall income.
- You become a more planned and strategic spender and less of an emotional spender. It becomes harder for people to take advantage of you, to "sucker" you into buying things, and to cheat you. You become a smarter buyer!
- Not only will you cover all of your needs, but if you have a family, you will cover all of their needs, too. You will not only become a better provider but you'll be less selfish in your spending.

A Snapshot of Your (Financial) Net Worth: Assets and Liabilities

Before getting to the actual budgeting, let's look at your assets and liabilities (what you have or own and what you owe).

Why would you want to do this before you work on your budget? Well, look at it this way. In this case, you are going to budget your money resources; you're going to organize your money into categories specifying what you must spend it on, what you'd like to spend it on, and what you should spend it on. Taking a "snapshot" of your financial worth, which is what all lending institutions do before they give you credit, helps you to first determine your goals and then how to budget your money.

Again, this process is similar to budgeting the time you spend on your career trying to become promote-able and in getting promoted. If you assess your career strengths (assets) against your career weaknesses (liabilities), you can then determine where you should budget your time.

Assets

Let's look at your assets. Justifiably, you may ask, "What are assets?" They are homes, cars, furniture, cash and cash accounts, tools and equipment, jewelry, investments, and retirement plans. They're expressions of how you live or how you want to live; they're things you enjoy and use now. Assets can also be sold, if necessary. Something that's important to remember: some of your assets may have little value, such as your computer, your TV, your stereo system, and so on. They become old or obsolete within a few months' time. They may have value to you, but they would not bring in much money if sold. Despite this caveat, they are still considered assets; just take this into consideration when valuing them.

Assets that you are most likely to have if you are just starting out include cash and cash equivalents. They consist of your checking account, your passbook account, your savings account (e.g., Thrift Savings Plan), Certificates of Deposit, Money Market accounts, and savings bonds. These assets are very safe and easy for you to turn into cash in the event of an emergency.

Some people are more experienced and skilled at investing and increasing their assets. If you fall into this position, then you may have some or all of the following assets: a house, other property, mutual funds, stocks and bonds, military retirement plans as well as the retirement plan in which your spouse may be participating (i.e., 401(k) plans, 403(b) plans, and 457 plans), etc.

Of course, these kinds of assets may not even be in your thoughts right now. However, remember that this book is meant to get you started on thinking about the opportunities that can be yours if you plan for them. Budgeting is simply the planning process that can help you gain more assets.

Let's now return to determining your financial worth. When adding up your assets, take care to inventory them correctly and to be realistic when placing a value on them. What do you have that is "sellable" and which of those assets can you sell for cash in a short period of time? Contrary to popular opinion, adding up your assets may become a pleasant task in that you may discover you have more wealth than you thought. Alternatively, it may also be a wake-up call if you find that you have less wealth than you expected.

Assets you may have if you are just starting out include:

Cash on hand	$_____
Savings account balance and savings bonds	$_____
Checking account balance	$_____
Thrift Savings Account	$_____
Car value if sold	$_____
Money owed to you (that you can actually collect)	$_____
Personal property you could sell	$_____
Cash value of your life insurance	$_____
Other assets (e.g., Certificates of Deposit)	$_____

More sophisticated assets you might have include:

Your home's value	$_____
Other real estate you own	$_____
Stock value	$_____
Bond value	$_____
Mutual fund value	$_____
Current cash value of retirement plans	$_____
Total Assets	$_____

Liabilities

The task of adding up your liabilities may be less pleasant than that of adding up your assets. To whom do you owe money and how much do you owe? For the purpose of this task, we are not talking about everyday expenses such as groceries, gas for your car, and utilities (electricity, gas, and phone bill). Those expenses are important for your budget, but they do not play a part in determining your net worth. The following are the types of liabilities you will need to add up when calculating your total liabilities:

Balance owed on your car	$_____
Credit card debt	$_____
Personal loans	$_____
Money owed to family and friends	$_____
Other liabilities you may have include:	
Balance of your mortgage	$_____
Balance of a second mortgage	$_____
Taxes in arrears	$_____
Other real estate loans	$_____
Total Liabilities	$_____

In determining your net worth, list your checking account, but do not consider your regular monthly income and expenses—these are cash transactions that may increase or decrease your net worth in the future, depending on how you budget your money. Your net worth is a "snapshot" of what you are worth right now and does not include these volatile factors.

A few quick questions: How would you determine your net military career worth right now? How would you evaluate your knowledge, skills, physical status, and latest performance review? How would you add up? Would you be an asset or a liability? How and on what would you then budget your time so as to become more of an asset to the military?

How Can You Increase Your Net Worth?

Now that you have determined how much you are worth (financially), let's look at how you will be able to increase your net worth and move down the road toward your financial goals via budgeting.
You can increase your net worth by:
- Spending less
- Earning more
- Making your money work for you

"Making your money work better for you" is more of a long-term savings and investment tactic. It will increase your net worth and you definitely should do it, but we will address this strategy later on in this book. For the time being, however, we'll focus on short-term savings and investment tactics.

There are just two ways to improve your finances in a short period of time: earn more money and spend less. It sounds very basic, and it is. It's easy, too. All it takes is for you to decide on your "money" goals, set up a budget to achieve those goals, and then have enough discipline to stick to that budget.

All of this requires discipline, but it's no different from your military life. And you already know you can do that well!

Setting Up Your Budget

It is common for people to spend all of the money they earn. Know anyone like that? Are you the spender who has nothing left at the end of the month and has nothing to show for all of your hard and sometimes dangerous work?

This scenario is true for military personnel and civilians alike. It is true for people who earn very little and for those who make a lot of money. In fact, many people have a tendency to spend what they make.

Moreover, most often, the problem is not how much you make. Rather, it's a question of where it goes and, frequently, you may not know where your money goes. This doesn't mean your rent or mortgage (if you have one of these), your utilities, and your car loan or lease. Those are necessities (although some individuals spend more on these items than they can really afford). You pay those items monthly and they are typically the same amount each month (or close to it). The real problem is the money you don't remember spending that adds up. In other words, the little things, such as fast food runs, on going out, on alcohol, on cigarettes, on clothing, or on cell phone bills.

When looking at the whole picture (your daily, monthly, and yearly spending and savings) look for areas that can be improved.

The process of budgeting includes tracking your income and your expenses, and then planning on how to increase your income (if possible) and how to cut your expenses.

Income: The definition of income is any regular payment you receive. A large, one-time payment, such as an inheritance or an insurance payout, would be considered an asset, not income. Your income includes your base pay plus any other pay you receive, such as hazardous duty pay, proficiency pay, sea pay, overseas pay, clothing allowance, basic housing allowance, and basic allowance for subsistence. These amounts all show up on the LES (Leave and Earnings statement) you receive at the end of the month.

Expenses: In determining a budget, it is critical that you do not underestimate what you spend. It is better to have a little left over than to have your money come up short at the end of the month. First, you add up all of your regular expenses; each expense should be calculated over the same period of time. (For example, if you pay your yearly car insurance in four installments of $400.00 each, this would amount to $133.33 per month [$400 divided by 3] for your budgeting purposes.) It's easiest to plan if you add up the monthly amounts you will be required to pay. Here is what your budget should include:

Income

Monthly net pay* $_____
Other income (i.e., spouse's income or second job) $_____
Interest and/or dividends paid in cash $_____
Child support $_____
Alimony $_____
Total Monthly Income $_____

*The amount of cash you have direct deposited after all taxes are taken out.

Expenses

Savings and investments	$_____
Food, health expenses, cleaning supplies	$_____
Mortgage/rent payment	$_____
Other regular home-related payments	
(e.g., maintenance and upkeep)	$_____
Auto loan/lease payment	$_____
Automobile expenses	
(e.g., gas and tune-up)	$_____
Credit card payments*	$_____
Other loans or financial obligations	$_____
Tax payments (if not taken from pay)	$_____
Insurance payments (e.g., auto, home, life, and disability)	$_____
Entertainment expense related to fun and family	
(going out—movies, dinner and drinks, birthdays,	
weddings and anniversaries, holidays and travel, etc.)	$_____
Utilities (gas, electric, water, and sewage)	$_____
Telephone (including cell phone)	$_____
Clothes and personal items	$_____
Total Monthly Expenses	$_____
Monthly Balance (Income minus expenses)	$_____

*Include the amount(s) that you regularly intend to pay. Do not include total balance unless you intend to pay off your balances every month. All credit card monthly payments should be listed separately.

Some Budgeting Tips

- Pay yourself first. You've heard that before, I'm sure. If you aren't already there, once you get to the point at which you have a positive Monthly Balance, put money into a savings plan, such as the tax-deductible, tax-deferred Thrift Savings Plan offered by the military. Develop a reserve or emergency fund for those unexpected expenses that will hurt or alter your budgeting attempts. Even if you only pay yourself $20/month, do so before you spend on leisure activities or buy something new. It bears repeating: pay yourself first.

- Moving on to your other expenses, remember, if you have expenses that are paid annually, biannually, or quarterly; divide the total amount to be paid by the number of months in the payment period to determine the monthly amount you owe. You must save that monthly amount every single month in order to have the money required to pay the larger, less-frequent bills.
- Your budget must be in writing. If you put your spending intentions down on paper it makes them more real. You become more committed to making your budget happen and, if you have a spouse, s/he can also see the plan and commit to it. It's hard to be part of the team if you have no idea where you're going and how you're going to get there.
- And remember, you must be realistic. Don't overestimate or underestimate your income or expenses.
- Be sure to include your entire regular expenses. Don't forget those expenses that you pay annually, bi-annually, or quarterly. Save an amount every month to cover the expense when it comes due. This technique will result in successful budgeting

Now that you have your budget, you may think that you don't have any money left over for fun. You don't want to give up everything you enjoy. If you do, you will not stick to your financial plan. How can you make the decisions you must make without giving up everything else in the process?

What happens when you fill in all of the blanks for monthly income and expenses and you have a negative balance? What do you do when your expenses are greater than your income? Things either have already or will soon break down for you and your family if this is a regular occurrence. Something will eventually give! You've got to have less going out than you do coming in; in other words, your income has to be greater than your expenses. How do you get there?

Increasing Your Income vs. Cutting Your Expenses

Staying in good physical condition is valued in the military, but how do you do that? You work out and you control your diet. What if you are working out a significant amount of time, however, and are still gaining weight? You must also eat right, the right types of foods and the right amount; you mustn't overindulge.

Getting in good financial condition involves much the same strategy. Your income is much like exercising and your expenses can be compared to your eating. In the military, you can only spend so much time on exercise and if you are still gaining weight you have to cut back on the calories. In the military, increasing your income is limited by a number of factors, much like it would be if you had a job as a civilian. Therefore, to get in good financial condition, you often have to cut back on your spending.

Let's take a closer look at this financial strategy.

Increasing Your Income

In the military, there are only a few ways to increase your income:
- Increase your time in the service;
- Earn a promotion;
- Be in the position to apply for and earn a Proficiency or Hazardous Duty status;
- Reenlist;
- Receive special duty pay; or
- Get deployed or obtain an overseas assignment.

Now in some cases, it may be possible to work a second job, part-time. However, military schedules make this possibility extremely difficult and military command typically frowns upon moonlighting.

Nevertheless, if you have a spouse, she or he can get a job to increase your family's income. But remember, her/his doing so is strictly to pay off your expenses and to get your debt down. It is not a strategy designed for going out and adding new debt and expenses to your existing ones.

Cutting Your Expenses

Cutting expenses is the opposite side of the coin. Most often, this is the best way to improve your budget situation. Keep in mind that these cuts should not have to be permanent. They will need to be maintained just long enough to get your budget under control. These cost-cutting decisions involve your real expenditures. You will have to give up something you want but may not need, such as:

- Restaurants/Fast Food/Takeout: Cook at home instead (what a novel idea!). It is so much less expensive to cook at home than it is to eat out. Think about preparing extra courses or servings when preparing meals. By doing so, you can save the leftovers and then, on a later day, your dinner is prepared when you get home from work. Fifty percent of the money Americans spend on food is spent on takeout and restaurants. By just packing your lunch instead of buying out, you will save a substantial amount of money.

- Look for the little things that might seem small to you, like saving one or two dollars a day. When added up, these single dollars could become a substantial amount over time. For example, you could eliminate that $2.50 "Cup o' Joe" you purchase on the way to the base each day. Just saving that $2.50 a day will add up to $625.00 a year. What can you do without? I mean really, think about the everyday expenses you have that are unnecessary. For instance, cable TV and all the possible premium channels—you may not have to give them all up, just part of them. The bottom line is: Tough situations require tough decisions!

- Shop for sales: If you insist on buying those name brands, wait until they go on sale, or go to the discount stores or malls instead. Think about it; are the name brands really better than the generic brands?

- Coupons: Coupon use can help you spend less. If you have children, think about getting them involved, perhaps splitting the savings with them as incentive. (As a bonus, this could become a good life lesson for them.) Coupons can be used for things other than groceries, such as gas, car maintenance, pizzas, dry cleaners, pet supplies, etc. By using coupons, you could see a savings of 10 percent or more on items you already buy. What is 10 percent of $300 (food, gas, pizza…)? $30 per month or $360 per year. Not bad, huh?

- Utilities are another area where you can save. By just turning off lights and turning down the heat or air-conditioning, you can save substantial amounts of money over time. Regulating the temperature of your home can be accomplished easily by purchasing an automatic thermostat.

- You can also save on insurance if you know the right questions to ask your agent. If you have an older car, for example, should you drop your collision coverage? Should you raise your deductible to lower your premium? Are you carrying too much insurance, or the wrong kind? Do you comparison shop when you purchase your insurance?

- Telephone/cell phone costs can really set you back, especially while you are away from your loved ones. What are you paying for? Are you carrying those fancy services that you don't need? Does everyone you know have your cell phone number? Do you use your cell phone unnecessarily? If you have a computer, use email. It's a great way to stay connected to your family and it's a lot cheaper than using the phone.

- See a credit counselor: You'll be amazed at how much they can help. They won't pay things off for you, of course; that's still your responsibility. But frequently, payment and interest arrangements can be worked out. What's more, if you can walk in and show them what you've been doing with this book, you'll score extra points.

- Pets can be expensive, especially dogs that need grooming every month. Either learn to do such grooming yourself or, when choosing a pet, consider what it will cost for its upkeep. If you are moved a lot or deployed, you may want to forgo the pets altogether.

- Gift giving can really get out of hand. Who are the individuals you "need" to purchase for? If you have a big family, you may want to draw names at Christmas and suggest no gifts for birthdays, etc.

Send a card with a letter in it; most of the time, this will mean more than a gift. Make a gift or send pictures. If you have large families to buy for, consider buying a family gift rather than a gift for each family member: a membership to the local zoo, a fun park, or the YMCA; gift certificates for the local video store; etc. Pool your money with other family members (i.e., mother, father, grandparents) and purchase one large gift, like a new TV, refrigerator, or dishwasher. Most of all think about the true meaning of the holiday. Bringing family and friends together is truly the best gift of all.

Shopping Tips to Assist You in Sticking to Your Budget

- Make a shopping list and stick to it. Reduce impulse buying and be less influenced by sales gimmicks and salespeople. Shop for groceries on a "full" stomach! You buy less if you're not focused on hunger.
- We tend to spend less if we go shopping with specific gifts and items in mind. It helps to watch for sales on the gifts you want to buy. Also, write down "who" is on your list; don't go buying for just anybody. Consider making your gifts instead of buying them; homemade gifts mean so much more to the person who receives them.
- Don't take your credit cards with you. The biggest budget buster is the use of credit; we will discuss credit and debt at length later in this book. If you have a spending plan and keep your credit cards at home, you will be less likely to overspend, or, heaven forbid, charge your impulse purchases. I know using credit is convenient, but with that convenience comes the danger of digging yourself into a huge debt hole.
- Keep track of what you spend. Check off the items on your shopping list as you purchase them and don't deviate from the plan. Keep a running tally of what you are spending. This helps prevent overspending because you'll know exactly how much you've spent. Always, always compare what you actually spent with the amount you have budgeted.

- Create a plan for spending. How much can you afford to save each month for holiday gifts? Set realistic goals. Perhaps you get caught up in the holiday excitement, because you have been stationed far away and have not seen your children, spouse, family, or friends in a long time. You want to bring them something, but if you can't really afford to, scale down.

Some More Budgeting Hints

- Cut one trip to the fast food restaurant each week.
- Serve one frugal (cheap) meal a week.
- Use store brands or generic brands instead of name brands.
- Use store and product/manufacturers' coupons.
- Try using the library on your installation or buy used books.
- Collect your checks and other bills for the last six months. Sort them by budget category, add them up, and see what you actually spent. You may be surprised.

Unexpected emergencies cannot be planned for, but if you expect the unexpected and put money away for expenses such as car repairs, home repairs, moving, and deployment in a special savings account, you will not have to use your budgeted money.

Remember that dining out and clothing expenses can get way out of control; be sure to budget a reasonable amount for each expense.

A budget is a plan and, like other plans, as situations change, so must your budget. You have to constantly review your income, expenses, and savings and renew your goals and objectives annually. You're in the service so you understand changing plans. You're flexible; you will adapt and overcome.

Budgeting requires self-control and discipline. With work and patience you will be able to have good budgeting discipline.

Break your strategies down. There are things you should do today, things you should do annually, and things you should do over the long term.

Things to Do Today

- List all of your regular income and expenses. Develop a budget and stick to it.
- Educate yourself. Check the newspaper, financial institutions, banks, and colleges. Community centers will often offer financial education for free. Take advantage of such information to keep up-to-date on the latest strategies.
- If you have a computer, use it to take advantage of a spreadsheet program that commonly comes with your computer. Having your budget on a spreadsheet will make the process much more manageable.

Things to Do Annually

- Review your budget. Include all of the individuals who are affected by your budgeting decisions. If you have a successful year, reward yourself.
- When your income increases, so will your ability to budget for the future (i.e., savings and investing). Don't let those increases fall through the cracks. Target those increases toward specific areas so they won't get lost in discretionary expenses.
- Review your insurance needs on a regular basis. As things change, such as you acquire assets or your family grows, you will need to increase your protection. More information on insurance will be found in a later chapter of this book.

Things to Do for the Long-term

- Unfortunately, as you, your family, and your children grow, your budget will change. Make sure you account for those changes; don't forget the dreaded college expenses.
- The budgeting decisions you make now will affect your future retirement needs. As you get closer to retirement, your budget will change. As retirement looms closer, medical expenses will most

likely increase. Be prepared! When you retire, your income and expenses may also decrease. Be sure to budget in some money for fun, travel, golf, hobbies, etc.

Now that you have your budgeting down, you will be able to plan for the various other financial areas of your life.

Chapter Two

Major Purchases

Money and Spending

Funny thing about money, we want it, we need it, we depend on it, we want to make it grow, and we want to spend it. Think about what money really is. It is a tool used in exchange for goods and services. It would be a very different world if we did not have money. We would live our lives differently.

As service men or women, money is what you accept from your government in exchange for your work. Money is what the cashier at the PX or the Commissary accepts in exchange for your groceries, shoes, clothes, TV's, and so on. We accept it from others because we know others will then accept it from us.

Money

Money is a form of exchange used all over the world. It is the function of two or more people agreeing to trade their resources for money with the understanding that they will be able to trade the money for something they want. It is the process of interchanging money for goods and goods for money.

Money is a regulated measure of value. You agree to the value of that money, for example: $1.00 is 100 cents. We price everything based on the dollar amount. When you have two items priced the same, they are equal in value.

There you have it; money is a medium of exchange to make trading easier. Since it maintains value from day to day, you can spend it at a later date. You worked very hard to earn your money; you should not view it as the most important thing in your lives, but respect what it can do for you if you use it wisely. It represents your time, commitment, skills, knowledge, and job performance. You should ensure that the results of your spending habits don't diminish the value of your work.

So, let's discuss spending the value of your money. We will discuss large purchases and how to plan for them and how to make the right decisions for you.

In this chapter we will cover:
- Transportation
- Housing: Renting or Owning
- College Planning: Your Children and You
- Other Large Purchases

Transportation

Purchasing transportation will be one of the largest buying decisions you will make on a regular basis. That's why it is important to take it slow when considering a new vehicle. This is not a time to allow your emotions to dictate your decisions.

Depending on your age when you start, you could buy as many as thirteen cars in your life. Because the prices of cars keep going up, each consecutive purchase will require a larger expenditure of your cash. If your first car cost $8,000 and the cost of autos rises at an annual average of 3%, your last car will cost over $55,000. That is if you don't upgrade. This means that over your lifetime you will have paid $348,000 just buying cars. That is a whole lot of money any way you look at it. More startling is the fact that this dollar figure doesn't include all of the other costs that are affected by your choice of car, such as gas, insurance, and maintenance.

In the first chapter of this book, we discussed budgeting and setting short-, intermediate-, and long-term goals. Transportation fits into the short category because of your personal (e.g., to visit family) or business (e.g., the military moving you from installation to installation) needs. In addition, because of these short-term needs, it may be necessary for you to purchase a car before you are financially ready to do so.

In this section of Chapter Two, Transportation, we will cover:
- Knowing your needs
- Researching before buying
- New vs. used
- Dealers
- Leasing vs. buying

Your Transportation Needs and What a Car Means To You

Think about what a car means to you:
- Is it just a means of getting from one place to another?
- Is it a form of status or prestige, or maybe even power ("my car's faster and louder than yours")?
- Is it a way of saying, "I'm a success"?
- Is it a way to attract the opposite sex?

Research

Have you ever known one of your friends to go out and get a car that was so hot? S/he loved that car! But then the car had one problem after another, and finally, your friend had to get rid of it. Perhaps that car was not only hot, but it was expensive, too. It turned out to be too expensive to keep, however, and your friend ended up getting it repossessed.

Given the possibility of the above scenarios, it just makes sense to take it slow and to do some research before you buy or lease a new vehicle. Visit your local library and review automotive magazines, or visit Web sites that contain tons of information on cars. From these magazines and Web sites you can determine vital information about cars, such as:
- Miles per gallon
- Maintenance or service issues, including costs
- Cost/price—dealer cost and sticker price
- How the value of the car will drop or depreciate over the next few years (This will affect your net worth—refer back to Chapter One for further details on this subject.)

- Performance ratings, which may or may not be important to you. It's great, maybe even awesome, that a car can go from 0 to 60 mph in five seconds flat. But where can you legally drive such a car without killing yourself, injuring someone else, or possibly putting yourself in trouble with your Commanding Officer?

While you are performing your search, you should also research the going interest rates for loans and leases as well as the typical number of years required to finance a car purchase.

Can you imagine going into battle or alert situation without having done any research about the enemy? Car dealers are going to try to get as much money as they can, through pricing, financing fees, and other "add-ons."

Research also allows you to be a better negotiator. If you know what other dealers can do for you, about the car's potential problems, and have an idea of what the dealer's costs are, you become a more educated buyer. Use Internet resources to learn more about your car purchases and to buy smarter!

Buying: New vs. Used

Should you buy a new or a used car? Many experts say as soon as you drive your new car off the lot, it's considered used and has already depreciated in value. If you can find a used car that meets your needs it is usually a better financial decision to purchase the used car.

When it comes to purchasing used cars, there are some very good deals out there. Because so many cars are leased today, there are many used cars on dealers' lots. These cars come back into the marketplace after two to four years when the lease terms are up. Dealers have these cars returning in bunches and they need to move them off the lot quickly. Some may still be under warranty, have low mileage, and have been taken care of by the dealer's service department.

Be very careful when buying a used car. Where you decide to buy the car is important. There are many car dealers and, with a little research, you should be able to find a list of reputable dealers that meet your needs.

Good used cars can be available at reasonable prices, but you have to take your time and search carefully to uncover them. If you find a pre-owned car from a private owner, you will historically pay less than retail for it. If you find a used car from a new car dealer, however, chances are you will pay close to retail, but you may also get a limited warranty.

Again, especially when buying a used car, do your research at the local library or through magazines. You should also check out the "blue book" value of the vehicle you are considering. This book contains the value of a good condition used car and the standard mileage such a car should have for the value listed. This information can be used in your price negotiations. If the miles on the car you are looking at are higher than the blue book specifies, then the price should be lower than the blue book's listed price. Also, check out the local Better Business Bureau to see if they have a profile available on any dealers you are considering.

Expenses to Consider When You Own and Operate a Used Car

Never purchase a used car without having your own mechanic inspect it first. That way, you'll have a list of problems to take to the dealer. This information will help you negotiate a reduced price for the cost of the repairs. Don't go through this process unless you have decided you really want the car. The mechanical inspection may cost you, but it's "pay now or pay later."

Used cars will likely require more repairs. Moreover, major problems can be expected in a few years, depending on how old the car is when you get it.

Since rapid depreciation occurs in the first two years of a new car's life, a used car will be less expensive if you are planning on owning the car for only two or three years.

Depending on the make and model of the vehicle you are considering, it may not be advantageous to buy some very popular, high performance used cars because they depreciate quickly. Check out the blue book value and educate yourself prior to the start of your purchase. A good strategy might be to start looking and researching before you need to replace the automobile you are currently driving. You don't want to have your car breaking down while you are searching.

Don't forget your automobile insurance costs. Check with your agent to see how your vehicle will affect your monthly expenses.

As with used cars, research is important when buying a new car. It can be particularly important to know what you need versus what dealers will try to sell you; forewarned is forearmed. Education is the key to recognizing the tricks, wiles, and ploys that may be part of their arsenal. You can beat them in their game and save hundreds, if not thousands, of dollars in the process. Do your research, don't become a hostage, and be prepared to walk away from a deal.

Remember, don't wait too long if your current car is dying. Even though you can't afford to buy today, start your research now. It could take as long as ten weeks to "kick" the tires, choose a car, check your credit scores, etc. Put the new set of numbers into your budget (don't forget the change to your insurance) and see what it does to your bottom line. Set up your financing, negotiate, and finish the deal. If you wait too long, you may be forced to make a quick decision, which puts you at a disadvantage.

Dealing with Dealers

Pull together information on the cars you like, their prices, and the dealers with which you want to work. Take that information with you and make sure the dealer sees it. If you take anyone with you, discuss the following items beforehand: no impulse buying and no disclosing what you are prepared to pay, even if the salesperson leaves you alone in the sales office.

Let the salesperson know that you've done your homework and that you know the dealer costs. You want to be fair, but you are not going to pay thousands of extra dollars. You also want to let the salesperson know that you are not willing to spend hours playing games. He or she will attempt to wear you down so that when you are tired, you will surrender. This strategy will also prevent you from spending too much time at one place, which might keep you from visiting rival dealers.

When dealing with an automobile dealer, keep the following tips in mind:

- Never, ever give them your ID card if they ask for it. Some dealers will use the information on it to run multiple credit inquiries with different financing companies before you have even decided to purchase a vehicle. If they will not let you test drive a car without it, go to a different dealer.

- Automobile dealers have a profit margin that is usually between 10 to 20 percent. That is the difference between the dealer's cost and the price you will pay.

- Negotiate with the dealer for a car she or he has on the lot instead of ordering a car. The dealer just might be willing to negotiate to get a car off the lot. You are more likely to pay less for a car that is almost what you want than you are for one that is everything you want. "I'd really rather have…" becomes "What can you do for me if I take this off your hands?"

- Don't let your emotions get in the way of making the best decision for you, both financially and practically. You will always pay more if you let the dealer know how excited you are about a certain car.

- Do not be afraid to walk out! This advice is very important; remember, some dealers have ways of keeping you in their showroom. Moreover, as you are starting to walk away, make sure you say that you "will have to check another dealer."

- Think about letting your fingers do the walking. By calling ahead of time, you will get the initial price information. You will be able to get competitive prices and you will not have to speak to a "salesman." If a dealer will not talk with you on the phone, you will know that s/he is not the person you want to deal with.

- To compare apples to apples, make sure the dealer quotes you the same figure (i.e., factory invoice price as a base).

- If there are factory incentives, you may be able to pay below factory invoice prices. You can sometimes go to the manufacturer's Web site to see the available deals.

- Always negotiate for the best price on the car. Don't negotiate monthly payments first; always negotiate the price of the car first.

- Be prepared to pay taxes, registration, licenses, and destination charges. Watch out for delivery, promotion, handling, sales charges, floor charges, or any other fancy items the dealer may use to get you to pay for things you do not have to pay for.

- Don't skip the test drive and don't just cruise around a few blocks playing the radio. During most of the test drive, keep the radio off and listen to the car; feel the car going around curves, listen to the engine, test its acceleration, and take it up on a freeway so you can test for vibrations at different speeds.
- Check things like the ease of ride, how easy it is to reach important controls, etc.
- Don't give the salesperson your driver's license; give him/her a copy.
- If your current car is broken down, don't drive it to the dealer. Borrow a buddy's car instead. Otherwise, the dealer will try to take advantage of your urgent need for another car.

When the conversation turns to financing, be aware that you do not have to use the dealer's finance companies. You can arrange for your own financing, which could help you avoid a higher APR. (See Chapter Five of this book for further details on this subject.) Always check with an experienced lending institution that regularly deals with the military near your installation, even to merely to discuss what the dealer is offering you. The dealer, on the other hand, well, sometimes that's a different story. Get information from the dealer, including information about any extra discounts, military discounts or rebates, student rebates, first-time buyer incentives, and so on.

Once the actual negotiations begin over the price of the new car, the salesperson will usually give you some ridiculous figure; he needs "to put you into the car today." Counter his offer with your lowest possible offer, based on the research and information you've collected prior to shopping. He will attempt to hold you there by going to "talk with his manager." Make sure he knows you will only wait 10 to 15 minutes. Don't be afraid to walk away. There are plenty of dealers and plenty of cars. You know what you should be paying, so you have the upper hand. Don't believe the sales pitch, "This is good if you make the decision right this minute." If the salesperson can offer it to you right now, for sure he can offer it to you until the end of the day, and typically longer.

Leasing vs. Buying

Once you have a set price then you need to decide on whether to lease or buy the vehicle. You may not know the difference between these two purchasing options, however. Many people think they can drive more of a car if they lease it instead of buying it. Leasing offers lower monthly payments, but in the long run, it could end up costing you more if you decide to purchase your leased vehicle at the end of the lease.

Here is how leasing works. You are leasing the car from a third party: the leasing company. The lease is based on the price the leasing company must pay for the car and the lease's money factor. There are other variables, such as the car you choose, the depreciation schedule (the resale value at the end of the lease), your down payment (you should think twice about a down payment on a car you don't buy), and state taxes.

Here are some things to think about if you are considering leasing a vehicle:

- Do you get tired of your car after a couple of years?
- Do you drive more than 12,000 miles in one year?
- Do you want smaller monthly payments?
- Do you take good care of your cars?
- Do you like driving a more expensive car than you can afford?
- Do you want to avoid the nuisance of trading in or selling a used car?

The advantages of leasing are:

- There is either no down payment or a low down payment.
- The monthly payments are lower than they are with an outright purchase.
- You can drive more car than you could typically afford to drive.
- Current tax rules favor leasing over buying if you use your car for business.
- You can purchase the car when the lease ends.

The disadvantages of leasing are:

- The mileage limits can increase the cost of driving by 25 cents per mile.
- Wear and tear charges can add up to be quite expensive.
- You're locked into a three- to five-year lease term and it's expensive to terminate early.
- There is no trade-in to help with your next lease or purchase.

Should you buy or lease? It's up to you. But please, get all of the facts before you commit to a final decision.

No matter what car you get, and no matter whether you buy or lease, before you make the decision, put the numbers into your budget. Doing so will help you evaluate whether this decision is good for you and your family (if you have one).

Housing: Rent or Buy?

Once you are in a financial position to buy a home, doing so can be a big decision for military personnel, particularly since you can move a lot and sometimes on a moment's notice. Therefore, service men and women may worry about selling their house when it's time to go. Frequently, civilians stay in the same community and have time to wait to sell one house before getting another. They can even place contingency sales terms in an offer. If this is the first time you are considering buying a home, talk to other military personnel (several) about the pros and cons of buying a home.

Buying a home may not be the right decision for you to make right now. You are in the military; there is a chance that you will not be in the same place for a long enough period of time to make buying a home an advantage. It takes at least two years to break even on the extra costs of homeownership. Those costs include mortgage closing costs, real estate commissions, and moving costs. In addition, you may have too much credit card debt or you may not have reached your potential income and, therefore, would not qualify for a mortgage loan just yet.

Some people rent because they like the flexibility or they've moved to a new area and are unsure as to where is best to purchase, based on neighborhoods, schools, convenient location to work and shopping, and so on. Moreover, many people just don't want the responsibility of owning and maintaining a home. It is important to make the best decision for you and your family. Take the time to list the pros and cons and the impact that buying a home will have on your financial well-being.

Why Rent?

When you rent, you agree to pay for the use of an apartment or a house for a specific period of time for a specific amount of money. Depending on the landlord of the property and the competition in the area for renters, you may not be required to pay a large deposit. (Before negotiating your rental agreement, find out what the competition is like and see if you can negotiate some free months or a lower deposit.) When you purchase a home, you could be required to have a down payment (up to 20%) plus closing costs. Some government loans or guarantee programs (VA or FHA) allow for smaller down payments.

Owning a home can be expensive. As a renter, you will not be responsible for maintenance of your building. If you own your home, on the other hand, you will be responsible for all maintenance and decorating, including but not limited to mowing your lawn, providing water hoses, tools, curtains, appliances (some appliances may come with the home), painting, fixing leaks, and so on.

When you decide to purchase a home, it is a long-term and expensive decision. The transaction can include:

- The real-estate agent's commission (unless you don't use an agent)
- Loan origination fees
- Legal fees (attorney)
- Taxes
- Title insurance
- Other paperwork

If you get deployed and are married, your spouse may want to return to his/her family while you are gone. In such instances, renting would work better for you, as it would provide more flexibility.

Renting may provide the freedom to move around as well. It might also suit your lifestyle better than owning. Ending a rental agreement and entering into a new one is fairly simple and can be accomplished quickly. Rental properties come in many sizes and price ranges and offer many amenities. Some even have fitness facilities, swimming pools, party rooms, etc.

When deciding whether to purchase, potential appreciation should be considered. The economy of the area, the property condition, and the school district the property is located in all play a factor in how much that property will increase in value. The down payment you save if you choose to rent could do better earning interest or accumulating in value in a Thrift Savings Account, a Certificate of Deposit, or some other investment opportunity.

Why Buy?

Buying a home will be your largest purchase. When you rent, you make payments, but you have nothing to show for it as far as value; you gain no equity (equity is the difference between the value of your house and what you owe), meaning you have no ownership in the property you are paying to use. As a homeowner, you may owe a large sum to your mortgage lender; however, since you do acquire an equity interest in the home, you can increase your value.

As a homeowner, you have more control over how your money is spent and, most importantly, homeowners can take advantage of tax deductions. The interest paid on your mortgage and the property taxes owed are deductible and can significantly reduce your taxable income.

There is something reassuring about owning your own home. You are not living under the rules of others or forced to behave in certain ways, other than the laws of the community. You have the option to decorate and use your home in any way you want. You will find that it feels great to call something "yours."

You need to spend a lot of time and energy educating yourself to make the best purchasing decision. If you think you have a lot of choices when purchasing furniture, cars, appliances, stereos, and televisions, hold onto your hat when you go to buy a home. A home purchase ranks right up there as stressful, scary, intimidating, and expensive. The reason is obvious: the big price tag! When purchasing a home, you need to make many decisions. Comparison-shopping will be tough because of the wide range of options available. At times, when comparing homes it will seem like you are comparing "apples to oranges to bananas to pears."

Price will be the biggest issue, when purchasing a home. How much will you be able to afford?

- Start with how much you currently pay for your housing.
- How much can you afford to shell out as a down payment?
- Over how long of a period do you want to stretch your payments?
- What are the current interest rates?
- Have you been pre-qualified for the loan?

Finally, a good rule of thumb is that your monthly payments for a house should not exceed 30 to 35 percent of your total regular pay. What is "regular pay"? It means to exclude pays and allowances that you do not receive on a regular basis. For instance, if, on average, you get Hazardous Duty Pay only two to three months out of the year, do not count it as part of your regular pay.

Five Mistakes to Avoid When Purchasing a Home:

1. Not understanding the role of your real estate agent. Most of the time, a real estate agent will be helpful and friendly and will want to do a good job for you. Her/his role is to shop for the right house for you. You will spend a lot of time looking for the right house, one that's in the right neighborhood and selling at the right price. Usually, an agent works for the home seller, unless s/he is an exclusive buyer's agent. Most states require the agent to tell the buyer whom they are working for, but just in case she or he doesn't inform you, ask.

    If the agent wants to work for both the buyer and the seller, it will result in a conflict of interest. You should hire a buyer's agent and work with her/him for at least 30 to 90 days. Be wary of anyone who insists upon an upfront fee or a long-term contract.

2. Don't fall in love (with the house!). If you love a particular house, don't show it! Don't wear your heart on your sleeve. And for sure, don't let the sellers or their agent know if you are simply dying to

own their home. If they find out, they could hold out for a higher price. You are going to go through negotiations; position yourself well by maintaining a noncommittal attitude.

Be smart by looking at a lot of houses. Know that if you take your time, you will find the one that will be best for you, your family, and their needs. Your dream home will become a nightmare if the monthly payments put you in the poorhouse. If you can't afford it, move on and keep looking. When you're ready financially, another "dream house" will appear!

3. Not doing the research and preparation prior to your search. This is where you need to get back to basics. What are your needs and how do your finances measure up? Remember your budget. If you're smart, you will analyze your assets and liabilities and pull your credit report before you start your house hunting. If you do the pre-work, not only will it save time but it will keep you from looking for a home that is beyond your means price-wise.

    Know the neighborhood. You are not just buying a home; you're buying a location, including the quality of its schools; its convenience to stores and your installation; its crime level; and its zoning issues.

4. Make a reasonable offer. Don't base your offer on the seller's asking price. Your agent should provide you with a listing of the market prices of the homes being sold in the area. This will reveal recent asking and sales prices of similar homes in the neighborhood. Armed with this information, you can make an offer that is comparable and typically better for you.

    Know what owning your own home means. You will soon have the responsibilities and costs of homeownership. You will not only have the mortgage payment, but also the property taxes, the repairs, and the cost of appliances, landscaping, improvements, and emergencies.

5. Not getting two important contingency clauses in the contract when negotiating. The first clause is a mortgage financing contingency clause, which saves you if the home does not appraise

for the offered price. Equipped with this clause, you can cancel the sale and renegotiate the price. Or, you can get back your deposit. The second clause hinges the deal on a professional inspector looking over the home and letting you know if it has any hidden flaws, structural damage, or faulty systems. If any are found, you may want to go back and negotiate or even back out of the deal. You may also want to walk through the house with the inspector to discuss what s/he finds.

Resale value and opportunities are vital if you are in the military. You do not want to purchase a home that you will have trouble reselling.

Purchasing a home will be one of the biggest investments you will ever make. So, take a moment to look ahead to the day when you will want to sell. Paying attention to the house's marketable details will go a long way toward preventing a big buying mistake. When your agent provides you with the market price history of houses being sold in the area, investigate how long they were on the market before they were sold.

College Planning: Your Children's and Yours

Saving for your child's education is ranked number two when it comes to major purchases in your lifetime. In addition, you may want to get a college education or a higher degree of your own. If you have no children and you've had all the education you want, this section may be of no interest to you. If you plan on having children or you currently have children, however, it would be in your best interest to read this section carefully.

First, let's take care of you. Is going to college a dream you haven't fulfilled yet? The great thing about being in the military is the opportunity to participate in the Montgomery GI Bill. This Bill was established to provide you with the opportunity to pursue a college education. When you first enter the military, $100 per month is taken out of your pay and is direct deposited into a GI Bill account for you. This money is only taken out for the first 12 months of your military service, but it yields a large sum of available money to attend college.

In addition, a Tuition Assistance program is available to you and you put no money of your own into the fund. This program enables you to go to college while in the military and covers at least 75 percent of your tuition. Certain requirements exist, such as the amount of time in service you must meet prior to taking advantage of this program. Also while in the military, after you meet your time in service requirements you may utilize some of the money from your GI Bill account to pay for books and to cover tuition costs not covered by the Tuition Assistance program. Make sure to check with your installation's education officer, however, for details on what is and is not covered.

When it comes to furthering your education, you may also qualify for other college funds that the military offers, such as the Army College Fund. This fund requires certain military testing numbers to be qualified. Finally, to understand what you may be qualified for and what you have to do to access the money, see one of your base Education Counselors.

Now, on to your children; one of the largest challenges facing parents today is planning, saving, and investing for their children's education. If you start early, college planning will look like retirement planning. You will use the same strategies and products, as well as some additional options that are available to you.

Time Frame for Planning

When planning for any major purchase, how much time you have between the planning and savings and the actual event is important. Remember, time can be your friend; the longer the time frame, the smaller the amount of money per month that needs to be saved. Obviously, just the change that happens when you have a baby will take some adjustments. You will find that your budget will need to be reevaluated and a savings plan will need to be set up for college.

Let's look at what options you have to consider when financially preparing for your children's college education:
- You will pay for the full amount of college.
- You will pay for part and your child will pay for part.

- You will not pay for any of the costs and your child will apply for Student Loans.
- You will have "rich" parents and they will offer to pay for their grandchildren's college education.

If you have decided to foot the bill yourself, it is critical to start saving now. Even starting before the child is born is a great idea.

There are many ways to fund college, but the one that has been marketed extensively over the last several years is the 529 plan (it's called this because it's covered by Section 529 of the IRS code), which varies in different states but whose rules are all the same. You or perhaps your parents (your kid's grandparents) set the plan up and name a beneficiary—the child. The owner of the plan can make contributions (as much as $55,000) the first year. (I know; wishful thinking on your part!) The owner of the plan will benefit from an upfront tax break on their state income taxes if they invest in the plan that is sponsored by their home state. There are no tax breaks offered by the federal government when the plan is first funded; however, the plan's funds are distributed tax-free provided that the investment is used for college costs, including tuition and room and board.

The bad news is, the law that allows the tax-free distributions expires in 2010, and if Congress does not expand it, the distribution will be taxed at the child's tax rate when distributed. This scenario is not as good as tax-free, but it's still a break nonetheless.

The funds in the 529 plan can be used at any accredited school of higher education in the country, including junior colleges. That is good news for you if you intend to remain in the military, since you have no idea where you will be living when your child becomes college-aged.

These plans offer a variety of mutual funds. (See Chapter Seven for more information on this topic.) A nice feature of most plans is an age-based option that keeps most of the money in stock mutual funds while the child is young. Over time, the plan gradually moves the money into less aggressive funds as the child gets older and closer to the time when the money will be needed. If you are not willing or able to monitor the funds over the years, the age-based option will be the best choice for you.

Keep in mind that very little money is required to set these programs up—around $15 in some states. A good practice is to target all monies received as presents for holidays and birthdays for placement into the college fund. Because the savings is gradual, you will be surprised how fast that money will grow. The real trick is to keep your hands out of the "honey pot" when you get into trouble. In other words, HANDS OFF!

For additional information on 529 plans, you can search the Internet. If you do plan to open a 529 account, it can be done directly through the state sponsor, your investment advisor, or your local bank.

The Coverdell Education Savings accounts work in much the same way as the 529 plans. Their distributions can be used not only for college, but also for private elementary and high school tuition and even for purchasing a new computer for school-aged children. Under this plan, you are limited to a $2,000 maximum contribution per year per child and you can pick the investment you like, just like you do with your IRA. The minimum amount required to open the account will vary, depending on the mutual funds you choose.

Some families set up an account in their child's name to invest for college. Minors, aged 1-18, depending on the state, are not permitted to own investments directly. As a result, UTMA (Uniform Transfer to Minors) or UGMA (Uniform Gift to Minors Act) accounts must be set up to hold such investments. Typically, a parent acts as custodian of the account, managing the funds on his/her minor child's behalf. Because the child is in a lower tax bracket, a tax savings on the dividends, interest, or capital gains exists. Several problems arise, however, if the parent chooses one of these accounts:

- The money ultimately belongs to the child and usually can't be shifted from child to child or from child to parent.
- When the child becomes an adult, s/he gains control of the money and, therefore, could decide to use the money for something other than college (i.e., a sports car, stereo equipment, or a trip to Europe).
- A well-funded custodial account could have adverse effects on the child's ability to get financial aid. Under current rules, a child's

assets are calculated at a higher rate when figuring how much financial aid will be awarded.

A great bonus you should consider when developing a college savings plan is that some companies will contribute to your child's education if you buy products from their companies.

Other Large Purchases

I realize that to some of you, a major purchase will be your computer, your stereo, your television, your furniture, and your appliances. The same strategies used in saving for a home or college will apply to these purchases; you will want to decide what you need and how much you can afford, and then you will want to research your options.

Choosing a reputable dealer will be half the battle. Too often, consumers are forced to deal with young, inexperienced retail sales clerks who don't know the product or who don't care if you find what you are looking for, or even if you ever come back to the store. You're military; you'll be gone before you know it, and sometimes before you can complain about the deal they gave you. Avoid this scenario by letting your fingers do the walking; check prices and models on the phone or over the Internet. When you find what you are looking for, only then should you make the trip to the store. Read, talk, and listen to whatever you can to become informed. Check with your friends and family, getting referrals from them to places where they bought items and were happy with their purchases.

Know the procedures for all repairs of your purchases; you will have options under a warranty or a service plan that may include home repair. If not, can the item be serviced locally, and what are the normal downtimes and guarantees? Check to see if the make or model is scheduled to be discontinued or updated.

Look at rebuilt computers, or go to the "scratch and dent" areas. These items will be cheaper, but most will have the same warranty as the others. Less-than-perfect items can be a great source of savings. There are certain things, however, that you should look out for when considering "scratch and dent" items:

- Make sure you check the item out THOROUGHLY! Most are sold "as is," so if they are missing anything when you get home, you're in trouble.
- Make sure you have a sales associate with you when you check out the appliance. S/he can verify that the appliance is not in good condition and/or does not have all its parts.
- Most outlet stores do not have delivery service, so you will have to arrange for private delivery or pick it up yourself. If this is the case, ask if they have an outside service that they usually recommend.
- If you do your homework and pay attention to sales and "bonus days," you will be able to save a lot of money.
- Some retail furniture and appliance stores have clearance centers at separate locations. Some are advertised while others are not. You could call the local stores and inquire about clearance centers. Another good resource for "next to new" and some brand new "scratch and dent" items is furniture and appliance rental stores. When you go to these stores, ask if they have used or "scratch and dent" items available for purchase. Sometimes they are updating their inventory and you can get good deals. You might also check the newspaper. A lot of times when service men or women are moving, they will not be able to or want to take their "stuff" with them. You can get great deals by taking these items off their hands.

Warranties

Generally speaking, you should consider the features and benefits of an extended warranty compared to the cost before deciding to purchase an extended warranty.

Extended warranties also don't cover the most trouble-prone years of an appliance's life. When an appliance, TV, or stereo has a failure, it tends to be either very shortly after it's put into use, or several years after it has been used. The time between six-months-old and five-years-old is usually the most trouble-free time in a product's service life.

Manufacturers give a one-year warranty on most appliances such as TVs, stereo equipment, computers, etc. They want to cover the immediate failures because those failures reflect poorly on their company. Extended warranty companies, on the other hand, know that if products make it past the first year, very few claims, and often no claims, will arise for the rest of the warranty's term. Moreover, most warranties don't cover a product beyond five years.

You may think that warranties are like insurance on your car, home, or apartment. That is not the case. Extended warranties are often sold as if they were a form of insurance. However, they're quite different, for these reasons:

- Extended warranties usually require a long term, such as one, two, or three years.
- They only cover the appliance itself, whereas car or home insurance often covers external liabilities.
- Extended warranties are usually not offered for the entire lifetime of an appliance.
- There is limited competition. You can price-shop warranty plans, but most people aren't aware of this.
- Warranties must usually be purchased when an item is new.
- Extended warranties have a poor cost-to-benefit ratio; they have a high cost with few benefits.

Find out from the equipment retailer whether you can get the warranty later on. Take your time without feeling any pressure to give it the consideration it requires to make the right decision for you.

Renting vs. Owning

If you are considering a "rent-to-own" company, it is important to consider all of the factors involved, including purchase price, interest rate, annual percentage rate, duration of the rental period, etc. The associated costs with these opportunities can be quite high in some instances. Some of these companies offer convenience, without credit checks, and don't require a long-term commitment. If you do the math, you will see that you may pay two to five times retail price. You need to look at total cost, not just the low weekly or monthly payment.

For example, a quote for a "rent-to-own" computer is $32.99 a week for two years, with a total cost of $3,431.00. Compare that price to buying a similar model with more power for $800.00. Just think; if you put aside that $32.99 a week for 24 weeks (less than 6 months), you could walk in and buy the same computer with cash.

Surveys show that people don't go to a rent-to-own store for price; they go because there are uncertainties in their lives. So, as a service member, you are a prime target. Rent-to-own transactions are not treated as credit because, technically, consumers don't own the item until they have made the last payment. Furthermore, usury laws don't regulate the fees you pay over and above the cost of the merchandise. If they were, consumer advocates argue, the consumers would see that they are financing their purchases at triple-digit rates. This payment strategy could put you deep in debt for a long time.

With rent-to-own transactions, customers make weekly, biweekly, or monthly payments for their merchandise. The interval is most often dictated by their paycheck. While companies don't check credit or ask for a deposit or a down payment, they will ask for several personal references and they will check your employment status. They will also check to see if the customer has ever skipped out on a "rent-to-own" agreement in the past. The skip rate is 1.5 percent. If you do decide to do this, be sure to read the small print: how much are the payments? Does the price include tax? Are there any add-on fees? When are the payments due? Is there a grace period? What are the late fees?

Also, check the contract to see who is responsible for broken merchandise or if the item is lost or stolen. Usually, it's the owner of the object, in this case, the store, who would be responsible. "Rent-to-own" agreements, however, often shift the burden to the person who is renting the goods: you!

What if the merchandise is a lemon: the computer crashes, the washing machine floods, or the VCR won't work? Most of the time, a store will bring a replacement "loaner" to you while the original merchandise gets repaired. If you expect new merchandise under such circumstances, then get it in writing with your contract.

Smart consumers read the contract completely before they sign. A better bet for consumers on a budget is to pay down your credit cards before taking on any more debt.

As you can see, for purchases that are large and small, it is in your best interest to: 1) evaluate your budget; 2) decide if you really need the item or just want it; and 3) realize that if you decide to purchase the item, you should pick the most cost-effective strategy. Do your homework, ask financial professionals to help you evaluate your choices, and be patient with your major purchases.

Chapter Three

Major Life Events

Your everyday life is going along and all of a sudden, you are facing an engagement, a wedding, the birth of a child, a relocation, change of station, or deployment. Frequently, people have not financially planned for these major life events. If unprepared, any one of these events could "put a dent" in all of the hard work you did to get your finances in order.

In this chapter we will cover the following Major Life Events:

- Deployment
- Relocation
- Engagements and Weddings
- Marriage: Love and Money
- Babies
- Divorce

Airmen, Marines, Sailors, and Soldiers recognize the need to be prepared with operational readiness and fitness for duty. Are you prepared for deployment? You bet! You're well trained, well equipped, properly fit, mentally tough, and so on. Yes, you can take care of yourself and your buddies.

But have you prepared your finances for your family, for the "battles" they may encounter while you're gone? Are they as well equipped as you are?

Deployment

As a service member, one major event that will affect you both emotionally and financially is deployment. So many areas of your life will change. If you are single, you will need to make arrangements with your landlord, your creditors, and your family. Not only will you experience all the emotions and relationship stresses discussed in this guide, but you'll also have the added burden of finding a reliable individual to handle your personal affairs during your absence. The importance of a will and a power of attorney is just as critical for single members as it is for their married counterparts

Do all that you can in the time you have after you are notified of deployment. If you are married, sit down with your spouse to discuss the effects your being away will have on your partner. Doing so can soften the blow, especially if your spouse does very little in terms of managing the finances. During your discussion, you should cover all of the basics, such as:

- How all of the financial records are organized;
- How to read the family budget;
- Any debts that are past due and how to deal with them;
- Which debts absolutely cannot be late and what can happen if they are;
- Whom to contact if a household emergency happens;
- For each account you have, whom to contact if payment problems occur; and
- Who and what office on the base, post, or station to contact for help.

Experts say that it's typical for spouses to undergo struggles when a military member is deployed. Furthermore, family finances often sit squarely in the middle of that struggle.

Communications and Financial Pitfalls

One issue with deployed service members is the worry about how they'll communicate with their family members about finances, childcare, family decisions, etc. during their deployment. To help ease these worries, the military provides free phone cards to deploying service members. In most cases, additional phone cards are donated by local businesses and citizens who want to contribute to military families.

Many installations also offer e-mail, video e-mail and videophones. Communicating about finances during the deployment solves a lot of problems down the road. The financial and separation issues have just created overlapping stresses, but talking through some of them with your spouse helps. Getting your military pay straightened out is the most important thing.

Deployed personnel serving in combat zones receive tax-free income, but the system is set up to withhold taxes as if it were ordinary pay, with refunds for the withheld taxes coming a few weeks later. It usually takes a couple of months to get those kinks worked out and the refunds coming back to the spouse.

Tax Breaks

Tax breaks on combat income are a real plus. They help the spouse back at home manage in keeping up with his/her expenses. The extra money you get back on the tax refund is a nice little windfall.

Even with the money saved on taxes, however, it's not that easy for deployed families to get by. Expect your spouse to visit with family and friends; this can cost more than you would normally budget. You may also incur additional childcare costs because you won't be there to share parenting duties. A simple dental appointment, for example, will require a babysitter since daddy/mommy won't be home to watch your children while your spouse is getting his/her teeth cleaned.

You can expect to have childcare costs even if you're a stay-at-home parent. The government helps out with affordable childcare at Child Development Centers located on most installations and with free childcare programs, such as the Air Force's Give Parents A Break.

Still, it's important that you understand that there will be extra expenses arising from your deployment. Don't make the mistake of thinking that your tax refund will cover them. You need to revisit your budget and keep a tight rein on your expenses.

The smart thing to do, if you can afford it, is to put some of the tax savings away for when the deployed member returns. Perhaps you can open a special savings account and attempt to put at least some of the tax refund into it each month as an emergency fund.

Reunion Planning: Return from Deployment

Special planning is needed when you or your deployed spouse return(s) from deployment. Don't plan on any big expenditures that first month after s/he gets home. You will not want to incur unneeded debt simply because you wanted to make up for lost time and celebrate her/his return. Expect the worst financial times to occur during the first two months of a deployment and the first two months after the deployed member returns home. Why? Because that's when all the bills start pouring in.

The good thing is that the family may actually have some money saved from the extra pay they received during deployment; the bad thing is you might be tempted to go out and buy a new car or something else and end up with additional new debt. The debt issue, coupled with the problem of deciding who now controls the checkbook, can create real problems. The non-deployed spouse has been taking care of finances and in comes the deployed member who now wants to take back that control.

It will be hard letting her/him have the checkbook back. It was probably hard to take over the finances if you were not doing them when your spouse was deployed, but now it's a struggle giving up that control.

Financial Checklist

- Plan ahead.
- Discuss what and when bills are due, where receipts are kept, etc.
- Have enough saved.
- Create a family budget.

Relocation

Relocating is a way of life in the military. The more it happens, the better you get at it. There are always costs affiliated with moving. Fortunately, most are covered by the military. Of course, if you live on base in the barracks, your cost will be minimal. If you live in base housing, rent an apartment or home, or own a home, however, there will be expenses involved.

If you rent an apartment or home and leave before your lease is up, you may forgo your deposit. You will then have to come up with a deposit at your new location.

Notify all your credit card companies when you move. A replacement card coming to your old address could cost you. Call the utility companies to turn off your service as well.

Try to avoid making large purchases just before or after your move. You need to get a handle on the cost of living in your new area. If you are married, your spouse might have to look for another job and your income will be affected.

If you have the opportunity to plan for the move, here is a timeline of how you should plan. (Remember, there are certain things you must do, things the military will do but you must initiate, and things you should check on. Find out from your command exactly what these things are.):

6 Weeks

- If the military is handling the relocation, find out exactly what is covered and what you're expected to do.
- If you have a house to sell, call a real estate agent and get it ready to go on the market.
- Start inventorying what you have. Determine what you can give away, throw away, or sell.
- Arrange for a garage sale.
- If you know how long you will be in your next location, consider renting.
- If possible, visit your new location and check out the area. You can use the Web to get a lot of information.
- Get a change of address kit from the post office.
- Make a list of everyone who needs to be notified of the move—relatives, friends, creditors, schools, doctors, dentists, veterinarians, newspapers, magazines, etc.
- If you're moving into temporary housing, consider arranging for a general post office address. It's good for 30 days from first delivery.
- Start a file for notes, receipts, and other details of your move.
- Start using food that's in the freezer.

- If you're flying to your new location, book your flight and arrange for the mover or someone else to ship your car. Arrange for a rental car if necessary.

5 Weeks

- Contact the Transportation Office or mover.
- Let the mover know how much packing you intend to do.
- Arrange for a storage facility in your new town if you won't be moving into a new home right away.
- Contact insurance companies to make sure your belongings are covered during the move. If not, find out what the mover covers. The company's basic insurance probably insures items by the pound, which is not enough. See what other insurance they offer.
- Have an appraisal of expensive items you want shipped by the mover.
- If you're moving into or out of an apartment building, reserve the elevator for moving day.
- Send change of address cards to the post office, etc.
- Notify schools, daycare, doctors, dentists, and veterinarians of the move and get copies of records.
- Cancel magazine subscriptions or have them forwarded to the new address.

4 Weeks

- If you're doing the packing, get boxes, tape, packing paper, and box markers.
- Start packing. Begin with things you won't need during the next few weeks.
- Pack a necessities box. This will contain stuff you'll need right away in your new home—dishes, utensils, a few pots and pans, coffee pot, can opener, towels, toilet tissue, toothbrush, etc. Make sure the box is clearly marked.
- Pack a separate box of cleaning supplies.

- If moving long distance, map out your route and book hotel rooms.

3 Weeks
- Check garage, attic, and other storage areas for items that need to be packed.
- Confirm with the post office that it has received notification of your address change.
- Be aware that movers won't take flammables, paint, ammunition, chemicals, etc. Refillable propane tanks must be emptied and sealed by a professional.
- Consider a sitter for children and pets on moving day.

2 Weeks
- Arrange to have utilities and phone service shut off. Be aware that movers need light, so have power cut off the day after you move. Keep phone services on through the move, unless you're using a cell phone. Don't cancel cell phone service. You may need it while en route to your new home. Arrange to have utilities and phone service set up on the day you arrive at your new home.
- Have the car checked for a long distance move.

1 Week
- Close any safe deposit boxes. Important papers, jewelry, etc. should be kept with you for the move.
- Defrost the freezer and clean the refrigerator.
- Refill prescriptions.
- Confirm the date and other arrangements with mover.
- You may want to close savings accounts, but keep checking accounts and CDs active until you can open up new accounts in your new town.
- Consider getting traveler's checks for the trip.
- Pack clothes and any items you're taking with you. Leave out only the things you will need up until the last minute.

- Drain oil and gas from lawn mowers, snow blowers, snowmobiles, etc. Return library books and movie rentals.
- Cancel newspaper subscriptions.

Moving Day
- Make sure someone's there to supervise the movers.
- After everything is moved out, make a final inspection.
- Review the bill of lading very carefully.
- Make sure the mover has a phone number to reach you in your new town. Set the thermostat at proper setting.
- Lock all windows and doors.
- If you're leaving appliances behind, make sure they're turned off.
- If the house isn't sold yet, make sure a relative and the real estate agent have keys.
- Let police know the house is vacant.
- Pack phones and other items you may have left for the last day.
- Don't forget the dog or cat.

Move-in Day
- Get there before the movers.
- Make sure utilities and the phone have been connected.
- Take a quick walk-around to make sure you remember where you want furniture placed.
- Someone should be available to direct the movers.
- It may take a couple of weeks to unpack all the boxes. Make sure the movers put them where they won't be in the way.
- Check for damaged items.
- Carefully review the bill of lading. Make sure all boxes and furniture are accounted for before signing.

Engagements

You meet the person with whom you want to spend the rest of your life. The time has come to purchase an engagement ring. Yikes! Isn't that expensive? The answer could be yes and it could be no.

Engagement Rings: Options

Buying a diamond ring is often an emotional and expensive experience. It does not have to be stressful and you don't have to go into a lot of debt to buy a nice ring.

There are as many ring choices as there are people interested in getting one. You can choose a stone shape that is round, oval, marquise, pear, radiant, emerald, heart, and princess, all with a variety of settings. Before you start educating yourself about carats and color, however, remember that there's more than one way to purchase an engagement ring. For example:

- You can buy the stone minus the setting.
- You can buy the setting minus the stone.
- You can buy the ring in a store that allows you to "trade-up" (applying the cost of the ring to a more expensive one, paying the difference).
- You can get engaged and forgo the purchase of an engagement ring altogether until you can afford what you want. (This may not be romantic, but it's practical.)

If you go for the practical approach, you might want to have an honest discussion about money and engagement rings. This is a great way to start dealing with sharing financial responsibilities.

Engagement Rings: Cost

If you are thinking about buying an engagement ring, the burning question will be: how much will it cost? That question is answered based on the quality and size of the stone you buy and the setting. Depending on what you choose, the cost can range from a couple hundred dollars to thousands of dollars. You'll hear the salesman say, "It's a gift for a lifetime," in an attempt to up your price range. On average, the amount you'll spend is equal to two monthly paychecks, but the actual amount you spend is a personal decision that only you can make.

Ideally, you'll have some money saved in the bank before you buy the ring or loose stone. Most jewelers will accept payment in cash or with a credit card. If you pay with a credit card you will have proof of your transaction. Of course, you will want to pay the credit card bill in full as soon as possible, so you will not incur long-term interest.

Engagement Ring Diamonds: The Four C's

As we previously discussed, you can buy a loose stone or one in a setting. When you choose a loose stone, you will be able to verify its quality with a report from an independent laboratory such as the American Gem Society or the Gemological Institute of America, both of which have established standards for grading a diamond's quality.

A grading report gives you a detailed description of the diamond, including its carat weight, shape, measurements, color, clarity, and cut. These are good things to know, especially if you intend to insure the ring, which is always a good idea. If your jeweler doesn't have a grading report, ask for one. If a jeweler hesitates or makes excuses, don't do business with him/her. The certificate you receive from the jeweler will also indicate if the stone has been artificially treated—fracture-filled, laser-drilled, or coated—to hide any imperfections.

A benefit of buying a loose stone is that you can customize the setting, such as having four prongs instead of six. With a loose stone, it is easier to rule out whether it is a fake—cubic zirconia weigh 55 percent more than real diamonds.

There are four characteristics (known as the "Four C's") that are used to determine a diamond's value: color, carat, cut, and clarity:

- Color: Diamonds become colored when elements such as nitrogen (yellow) and boron (blue) mix with carbon when the stone is formed. Colorless diamonds are rare and, therefore, more expensive. The GIA (Gemological Institute of America), which established color grades, considers D diamonds colorless and Z diamonds the most yellow.
- Carat Weight: Technically, this is the stone's weight, although it's used to refer to its size as well. One carat is one-fifth of a gram or 1/142 of an ounce. A carat is divided into 100 points, so a ½ carat diamond is 0.5 carats.

- Cut: This term refers to the diamond's proportions, symmetry, and finish (also referred to as polish). How a diamond is cut affects how much light the stone reflects—the better the cut, the more light the diamond reflects (thus giving the stone "brilliance" and "fire," as jewelers like to say). In fact, the AGS (American Gem Society) estimates that a diamond's cut can affect as much as 25 to 50 percent of the stone's value. A round brilliant diamond is an ideal cut and the most valuable—only 5 percent of the round brilliant diamonds in the world are cut to this standard.
- Clarity: This term refers to the presence or absence of flaws (the industry term is "inclusions") in the diamond. The majority of diamonds have some minor flaws, most of which are only visible with a magnifying glass or jeweler's loupe. Both the AGS's and the GIA's reports include a drawing of the stone that shows the size and location of any inclusions.

Diamond Clarity Grades:

F	Flawless
IF	Internally flawless—minor surface blemishes; none internally
VVS1, VVS2	Very, very slightly included
VS1, VS2	Very slightly included
S11, S12	Slightly included
11, 12 and 13	Imperfect; the inclusions are easily visible

Engagement Rings: Trade-offs

After you choose the shape and settings, the fun begins. Considering your budget, is size or quality more important? Retail jewelers nationwide sell diamond engagement rings that range from 0.20 carats to 1.50 carats, from color grades of G to I, or better, and from clarity grades of S11 or better. According to *Rapaport Diamond Report*, an industry publication, "Go for [color] grades H or I. Once mounted, they'll look just as good to the average person as the higher grades, without costing a bundle."

Engagement Rings: Quality Control

In addition to his/her professional experience, a reputable jeweler will have a written return or guarantee policy, which might include training from the GIA as a Graduate Gemologist or an Accredited Jewelry Professional or from the AGS as a Certified Gemologist Appraiser or a Certified Jeweler.

You should feel comfortable asking questions and taking the time you need to make a decision. When you buy a loose stone, be sure that important details about it, such as color, clarity ratings, and weight, are included in your receipt.

Finally, negotiate the price. Most retailers dramatically increase prices. Never pay the sticker price unless you've shopped around and you know that they are giving you the wholesale price.

Prenuptial Agreements

No, you're not a movie star or rock star. You're not a wealthy corporate CEO; nor are you royalty or any of the other types of people whom you might think would normally want a prenuptial agreement.

Prenuptial agreements, however, are not just for people who are rich. A person who has managed to save assets totaling $10,000, $20,000, $30,000, or more may want to be protective of their nest egg as much as someone who has millions. It takes hard work to accumulate any amount of wealth. You may want to consider a prenuptial agreement if you fall into any of these categories:

- You have assets such as a home, stock, or retirement accounts.
- You own a business or part of a business.
- You have children or grandchildren from a previous marriage.
- You anticipate receiving an inheritance.
- One of you is wealthier than the other.
- One of you is supporting the other through college.
- You have loved ones who need to be taken care of, a disabled child, or elderly parents.

As cold-hearted as it may sound, financially protecting yourself prior to getting married may be the smartest thing you can do.

The Wedding

Now that the ring has been purchased, the fun begins! With the excitement of being engaged, it's very easy to be swayed by all of the beautiful items that are presented to you. In other words, it's easy to forget that you are the consumer and that your money will pay for all that will go into making your wedding memorable. If you were making any other big purchase decision, you would weigh the options carefully. You would check all of the resources available and you would compare prices. Do the same thing with your wedding.

How do you have a beautiful wedding without going into the poorhouse? You want a lavish wedding and you want to invite everyone you know to the fairytale event, but can you afford it? Well, you can have a beautiful wedding; you simply need to decide to save as much money as possible beforehand. Let's look at one way of having a great wedding that you will be able to afford.

Forming a Budget Plan

Although most people arrange a wedding from a budget, drawing up a realistic plan can be tough. One place to start is to look at how much you currently have available to spend and what you want to spend. Look at an amount you can afford without the help of relatives. That way, you will have a more realistic notion of how much you will have to spend. Not having relatives involved at this point can be a bonus. No one else will be able to call the shots by threatening to withhold money. Of course, I am not suggesting that you turn down money if offered. Most of the time, relatives chip in at least some cash and, of course, will have requests in return.

No matter how much you decide to spend, you should first decide together, as a couple, what kind of wedding you want. You will have to compromise and ask questions so that you will know your fiancé's priorities and values. It will help you know what kind of wedding s/he would like to have. When you make those decisions privately, you will need to stick with them publicly. You will want to show a "united" front to the world. Doing so will make it harder for friends and family to talk you into something you don't want or can't afford.

Okay, now that you've set a realistic budget—let's say $5,000—what can you do to stretch those dollars as far as you can?

- Choose a time of year that is slower. (May, June, July, and September are the busiest months for weddings.) In January, February, or November, you can pretty much set your price. Wedding-related services will wheel and deal when business is slow.
- When choosing vendors, look for a smaller company that does not have a lot of overhead expenses. Ask around; see whom friends and/or family members have used in the past. Don't hesitate to negotiate. You will be surprised how much you can save by negotiating.
- Never forget you have the money; make vendors earn it. Get estimates from at lease five vendors per category: flowers, photography, clothing, the reception area, and caterers.
- When dealing with photographers get a price. Photographers tend to deal in "packages" and don't want to give prices for non-packages. Don't let them sell you a bigger, more expensive package than you need. If you purchase the disposable cameras, one for each table, you will be surprised how good the pictures turn out. Allow your guests to take pictures during the reception rather than paying a photographer to do so. You will have wonderful, non-posed pictures for a lot less money.

The Wedding Dress

The wedding dress is the one of the largest, most important costs in a wedding, but it seems to be the one item for which couples do not shop around. There are several reasons to shop around; some bridal shops will take tags off of the dresses so you can't get the information needed to look for the dress at other locations (i.e., Internet, discount stores, outlets, etc.). In that case, you can still get a picture, or at least try to. (Some shops will not let you take a picture.) If that is the case, write down as much as you can about the dress. Look at wedding magazines; if the dress you want is a current style, you will likely find it in a magazine.

If you still can't find the dress you want, consider contacting a DBS (Discount Bridal Service) consultant. In many cases, DBS consultants can save you 10 to 30 percent; just shop around. The idea is to comparison shop. There are many resources on the Web that will enable you to do so. Use your search engines to assist you. Wedding planning can be an emotional time; try to keep your buying levelheaded.

There are always alternatives to shopping retail. You will find many outlet stores that sell wedding and bridesmaids' dresses. Wedding-specific rental shops are also increasing in number as the popularity of renting a wedding dress grows. (Let's be realistic; you will never wear the dress again and if you plan on your daughter wearing it when she gets married, realize that statistically that will not happen.)

Consignment or thrift shops will sometimes carry "slightly" used dresses that are only a few seasons old. Some dress styles are ageless, so this may not even be a factor. Although such shops often include older gowns, you may find that the styles from the 1960s and 1970s are very similar to today's styles as fashion trends often repeat themselves. These shops will also sometimes throw in the veil for free; all you need to do is ask.

Don't be afraid to borrow from relatives or friends. They will be honored that you asked. Speaking of friends and relatives, whether it's a cake topper, a cake server, or their skills in cake making or flower arranging, they will be happy to help out or give you their services as their wedding gift.

When shopping for items that are not obviously intended for a wedding, just don't say the word wedding when negotiating! Mere utterance of the word wedding causes prices to rise. Put this to the test. Call the location where you are looking to hold the reception. Tell them you are planning a family get-together and get a quote. Then have someone else call and get a quote for a wedding reception. You will probably see a 25 percent increase in cost between the two scenarios.

Another example of this is craft stores. If you look for "Bridal Pearl" strands, you will find their cost is about $2.49 for 10 yards, while the same pearl strands in another section is 99 cents for 25 yards. Likewise, if you're looking for bridal brocade, you will pay $28 a yard while the same fabric is sold in the upholstery section for $13 a yard. It's unfortunate, but when you associate an item with a wedding, you will often find that the price goes up.

Remember that the Internet is your friend if you are looking to save money on your wedding. There are many sites that can help you obtain the information you need to reach your wedding goals.

After reading all of this, eloping might be starting to sound good. It's a very low cost alternative and you can always have a nice party to celebrate your nuptials after you return.

Marriage: Love and Money

What a wonderful feeling! You just got married and are looking forward to the years of sharing your love, your life, your checking account, and your debts. Wait a minute; bet you weren't thinking of those last two items!

The most common reasons people find themselves in a financial jam are poor planning and lack of communication. Too often, couples live for today with little regard for tomorrow. Couples don't talk about money and their financial goals. Rather, they commit to multiple long-term debts and hope for the best.

Start with the simple decisions. For example, how will you manage your cash and savings? Most couples merge their money into a joint checking or savings account when they get married. The reasons for doing so vary from being able to keep better tabs on the cash flow to reinforcing the feeling of two people becoming one. Some marriage counselors, however, say that the decision to take joint accounts should not be so cut and dried because each person brings a different set of money habits to the table.

"Becoming one" means knowing the other person—really knowing—before the wedding day. You could use the time between the engagement and the wedding to observe each other's financial habits. For instance, is your fiancé a "big spender" or does s/he account for every penny going out of the household?

The bottom line is that the rules are pliable and can be custom-fitted for any couple. And remember, you are in the military. It is very likely that you will be deployed a number of times during your career. Because of deployment, service men and women especially should have equal knowledge of and responsibility for all of their financial dealings. So, start laying the groundwork right at the beginning.

Adjusting to Changed Status

You may think that you're ready to make the transition from using your checking account to buy a new wardrobe on a whim to putting that money toward your married-couple expenses. Remember, however, that everything now becomes a joint decision. You are making decisions that affect each other's money. Instead of "I deserve those stiletto heels" or "I deserve those CDs," the story becomes, "Can we afford them?" or, even worse, "May I buy them?"

The whole process of moving one's money from an individual account to a joint account is pretty standard. If both parties have their accounts at the same bank or credit union, the first step is establishing a new account, or closing an existing account, and merging the money into another existing account. If you are closing an account, be sure you leave enough money in the account to cover any outstanding checks.

If you want to close your checking account and move your money into your spouse's account, fill out an application listing personal information, such as address, employer, and how much will be deposited. The decision of who will be the primary account holder then needs to be made. Some banks aren't set up to allow two people with different last names to have separate checking accounts linked to a joint savings account. Check with the bank of your choice to see if they have unusual rules. Adjusting your bank account is only the beginning!

Team Financing

Developing money habits as a team is one of the biggest adjustments newlyweds will ever make. The hardest part will be deciding how the money for daily expenses and savings goals will be handled. We will discuss the easier part, setting up the account to reflect the cash flow. The hard part is then up to you!

Generally three different financial options are available for couples:

1. One joint checking account—With one joint account, both parties deposit their paychecks into the account from which all bills can be paid. This way, both individuals know where they stand as a couple and it's often easier to be budget-conscious. In addition, one account will make for easier bookkeeping and bank account fees can be kept at a minimum.

2. Two personal checking accounts—On the other hand, some couples feel restricted by having one joint account because neither has his/her own money. While it's easier to manage a joint account by using just one checkbook, bad feelings may be alleviated if the couple uses two checkbooks. The former option could pose a real problem, however; not only does it require discipline and the agreement of both parties to keep good records, but it is particularly hard if one of the parties is in another city or country (which happens when military personnel are deployed). The problem will often lead to heated arguments. Using two personal accounts is often a good choice when one of you travels extensively.

3. One joint account and two personal accounts—A couple who chooses to have two separate checking accounts may decide to use one checkbook from either of the accounts if expenses are divided right down the middle. Finally, a couple may opt to have one joint account and two separate checking accounts. The majority of money can go into the joint account to pay daily living expenses. The remainder is divided between two personal accounts. The positive side is that you have your own money to control as well as some joint cash. The downside is that if you are not careful about saving, this system makes it easy to cut into your joint goals. That's because you're feeding two accounts, making it harder to save. Also, this last system costs you the most because you have to pay bank fees for three accounts.

Babies

Babies are wonderful and cute, but they are also costly. You will see a huge impact on your finances once you have a baby. Your goals and objectives will change, your budget will change, and your income may change.

Your time frame to have a child may be planned but sometimes it just happens. Having a financial plan set in place prior to the blessed event is suggested because when the baby arrives, you will find that your focus may shift. Also, you will find that you will not have the time or energy to get your act together.

When you are planning for your child, the first area that you should address is insurance, specifically life insurance (see Chapter Eight of this book for more information about insurance). An important point to remember is that you will need to make sure that your spouse and children are taken care of if anything should happen to you. If there are just the two of you, life insurance may not be as pressing, although it is still important if you have debt you would not want to leave your spouse with. With a child, however, you will want to protect and insure for her/his care until s/he is 18 years old, including education and college costs, etc. (see Chapter Two, Major Purchases, of this book).

You should also plan for childcare. You need to decide whether or not either you or your spouse will stay at home with the child. Obviously, if you are in the military, you do not have that choice.

If the baby comes sooner than expected, your career may be interrupted or you may decide to work part-time. Any way you look at it, your expenses and budget will be affected.

When you return to work, childcare will be required. Most bases have childcare facilities, but they are only open during the day. This may pose a problem if you are a single parent and are a shift worker. The cost of childcare can be expensive; you may pay $230.00 (on installation) a month per child or about $2,760.00 a year, or even more if you use an outside center.

New babies mean other expenses as well. You will have diapers, formula, and clothing to think about. You will enjoy planning and preparing the nursery, buying clothes, and stocking up on supplies. Many first-time parents suffer from "sticker shock" when they begin purchasing the needed baby accessories. It's natural to want all of the latest gadgets and adorable clothes. Be careful, however, because these expenses add up quickly. Remember that many items will only be used for a few months so consider purchasing from family, friends, consignment stores (e.g., second-hand baby stores), or yard sales. The only item you should not buy used is your car seat. That's because it is impossible to tell just by looking if a car seat is damaged.

As you can see, babies take planning:

- Make a will if you don't have one and adjust the one you have if you do.
- Make of list of the things you want to purchase.
- Figure out how much you will want to save by the time your baby is born.
- Reevaluate every two months until the baby is born to catch anything you missed.

Waiting for the arrival of a new baby is an exciting time. New moms enjoy preparing the nursery, buying clothes, and stocking up on supplies. New worries also creep up, like how to make ends meet once maternity leave begins and the family expenses increase. One strategy would be for the parents to decide to live on one income and to start saving now for the months ahead. A new baby can stress financial family life but this doesn't have to be the case. Careful planning, sensible choices, and a willingness to hunt for deals can reduce financial strain and make the arrival of a new baby the joy it is supposed to be.

Shop at Consignment Stores or Second-Hand Stores

Consignment stores that specialize in children's items are a godsend for savings. One good thing about babies is that they are gentle on the things they use. Cribs, high chairs, portable playpens, baby monitors, car seats, and strollers can look almost new even after a previous owner. Clothing is the best deal around because most babies will outgrow their clothes before they wear out. Buy diaper shirts, sleepers, booties, socks, and hats to start with. Be careful not to purchase too many clothes in newborn sizes, as they won't fit within a few weeks. Don't forget to pick up a rattle or two.

Shop at the Exchange, Commissary, or Large Chains

If you don't like consignment items or don't have a store near you, stick to shopping at the Exchange, Commissary, or larger chains and club member stores. Keep your eye on the weekly flyers for sales in your area. Most large chains have "baby week" sales. If shopping for clothes in department stores, buy at the end of the season. For example, if you are having a winter baby, shop for some 18-month-sized summer items at the end of the summer. Buy nursery staples such as cotton balls, petroleum jelly, baby shampoo, and diaper rash cream as you see them on sale at the supermarket or drugstore.

Things You Don't Need

Some baby items are not necessary on a tight budget:
- Baby swings are only used for the first four months, so try to borrow one if your baby likes to swing.
- Fancy crib toys are a waste of money. One or two things in a crib are plenty.
- Not having a changing table is a livable situation.
- Bassinets look pretty but they aren't used past the first three months.
- Babies don't need lots of toys. They are more interested in the world around them and with everyday objects.
- Forgo using baby wipes. A wet washcloth is much cheaper.

Borrow or Exchange Items with a Friend

Ask around for what you need and you may be surprised what people are willing to give away or loan. It may seem embarrassing to ask for hand-me-downs or second-hand items, but the money you save is well worth it.

Many thrifty women wonder, "How can I resist the little outfits and accessories?" Nine months is a long time to resist a spending spree. Here are some tips that will help you spend wisely:

- Wait it out. Once the pregnancy test indicates "positive," forgo the urge to go out to the store and pick up a giant bag of diapers.
- Collect coupons. Keep your eyes open for coupon deals on diapers, formula, baby toys, etc. Stock up at sales. If you know a pack of diapers is regularly $10.00 and they are on sale for $5.00, feel free to stock up. Match coupons to save more.
- Go online. Sign up for baby newsletters and join free parenting Web sites. The newsletters will not only keep you updated on your baby, but they will also inform you of deals and discounts.
- Inherit baby items. Ask your family and friends if they have baby items, such as strollers and cribs, which are in good condition. Be sure all items meet safety standards.
- Buy after your shower. Babies bring out people's generosity. Wait until your shower, which may not be until the 3rd trimester, to buy baby items.
- Spread the word. Let your family and friends know that you are hoping to get diapers, formula, etc. Having these necessary items on hand will free up money in your future budget.
- Register for gifts. While some may question the etiquette of baby registries, it's up to you to decide what's right for you. There is no better way to let others know what you need so you don't receive what people think you need or duplicates, such as 50 baby grooming kits.
- Your nursery theme. Resist the urge to buy everything that matches the theme. If they sell a bathtub that matches your theme but isn't very good quality, buy a generic bathtub that has the right features instead.
- Here is the most important tip of all: All your baby cares about is being loved, wearing a clean diaper, and having a full tummy. When expensive toys and outfits tempt you, remember that it doesn't have to cost a lot of money to raise a happy and healthy baby.

Divorce

Statistically, for every 1,000 marriages, about 550 divorces take place. More than one million children are affected by the million-plus divorces each year. Based on those numbers, a lot of families are trying to answer this question: how can we get through this process with the least amount of stress and not have it impact our finances?

Before we start, let's agree on our goal. Divorce is a controversial topic for society in general and on a personal level for those involved. We're not going to discuss either of those issues. Rather, we'll try to provide some information so that couples that are considering divorce can look at their budgets and have additional information at their disposal to make a decision that's best for their situation. In an emotionally charged atmosphere, having the right information is vital.

In most cases, the total cost of supporting a family increases during and after a divorce, while income and assets remain constant or decline. Therefore, the standard of living goes down. Some major decisions are required when contemplating divorce:

- What to do with the home
- How to distribute the property
- How to divide retirement assets
- Spousal support
- Child support

Divorce can take a household from middle or upper class into poverty. The standard of living for the family will be affected to a great extent. With the high number of divorces, couples need to try to work things out to the benefit of both parties. The problem is that emotion often gets in the way of common sense. When that happens, money mistakes can happen.

Divorce is ranked number two when it comes to stress in people's lives, mostly because it involves so many drastic changes—it entails emotional, social, and financial changes. Most of the time, these aspects can't be avoided.

In households where there are very few resources, both parties are adversely affected by a divorce. Many couples have a lot of debt in credit cards, etc. They were struggling before deciding to divorce and things can only get worse. In fact, a large percent of individuals getting divorces cite financial problems as the leading cause of their marital demise. Furthermore, those financial problems will only get worse, not better.

Unlike the settlements of even ten years ago, when alimony provided some cushion from financial devastation, less than five percent of today's divorce settlements allow for any type of alimony. Because of this statistic, women seem to be affected more than men are. Insufficient child support is another major area of financial hardship.

Legal fees are large expenses; retainers for each spouse can range from $1,000 to $5,000. Factor in additional charges and expenses, and legal fees can go even higher, depending on how long and drawn out the process is. There have been couples that have decided to stay together because they could not afford to divorce.

Here are five common myths about divorce:

1. *Everything will be split 50/50.* Every state is different; there are a number of factors that are taken into account when the division of property takes place.

2. *No-fault divorce is quick and painless.* All divorces involve negotiation over the disposition of assets and the care and support of children is an integral part of the process. None of this is quick or painless.

3. *S/he will have to give me support.* Today, most divorce settlements do not include any spousal (husband or wife) support. Alimony is generally awarded to older women in long-term marriages who have never worked outside the home. Some short-term alimony may be awarded until the spouse can find or train for employment.

4. *The wife should get the house.* This could be a mistake. The wife usually thinks that if she maintains the house, the children will be less affected if they do not have to move. The wife may find, however, that she is unable to afford the mortgage, taxes, and maintenance on the home with just her salary. This can be the same situation for the husband, even if he is the primary breadwinner.

5. *I'm not responsible for my ex-spouse's debt.* If you have jointly held credit cards and loans as a married couple, you are responsible for half of that debt. Creditors expect to be paid by both of the parties who incurred the debt. If you are contemplating a divorce, you should close all jointly held open-ended credit lines, such as home equity lines of credit and credit cards. You should then notify existing creditors in writing of your impending divorce.

Most importantly, consult an attorney, ask questions, and, if in doubt, get a second opinion.

Chapter Four

The Cost of Borrowing

"Hey, we have liberty tonight; can I borrow some cash 'til we get back to home port?"

"Say, I'm having trouble with my car; can you lend me a few bucks 'til we get paid?"

Whether you're doing the asking or you're doing the lending, most service men and women don't fully understand borrowing. The "cost" of borrowing from each other can be the loss of friendship and the loss of trust. If done often enough, it can mean a bad reputation and lots of harassment.

Borrowing money—whether it's the use of a credit card to purchase something, a debt consolidation loan, borrowing to buy that diamond ring, a stereo, or a car, or getting a second mortgage to replace your furnace—requires that you typically pay back more than the original cost of whatever it is you are buying.

Yes, that's right! If that stereo's sale price is $1,000 and you take out a loan to buy it, you may end up paying $1,200 (more or less, depending on the interest rate, annual percentage rate, and other applicable fees and on how long it takes to pay it off).

An interesting concept arises here. You can't afford to buy something with cash today, so you spend more money than it's worth.

If you can't afford it, don't buy it. Now there are obviously certain exceptions to that rule, such as the purchase of a house or car. There are also certain emergencies that, if your emergency fund doesn't cover the need, such as a furnace, you may have to borrow money for the safety of you and/or your family. If your stereo quits working, however, this may not be an emergency!

Nevertheless, there will be times during your life when you will borrow money. The next two chapters will cover:

- Credit Cards
- Loans
- Interest Rates & APR; and
- Bankruptcies

All of these topics deal with the "cost of borrowing." Self-discipline is necessary to prevent and manage (if necessary) the high cost of borrowing. Financial institutions are not helping when they offer you high-limit credit cards, five-to-six-year car loans, and large home equity loans with very moderate repayment terms. All of these offers make it hard for you to say no.

Service men and women are often treated just like college students by credit institutions: great marketing targets for credit. With college students, the lenders figure mom and dad will make good on the debt. With Airmen, Marines, Sailors, and Soldiers, they figure if you don't pay off your debt yourself, they'll ultimately get it out of your paycheck through enforced allotments.

Many people think credit is a quick fix for their problems. The truth is, improper use of credit frequently turns short-term financial dilemmas into long-term problems, which results in high-cost difficulties that can seem never-ending.

You end up with the worries and stress of making those payments on a limited military income. And then, if you're like some military personnel, you end up leaving a job you love to look for "greener grass." Once there, you find that not only is the grass not "greener," but because you didn't really resolve your previous financial problems, you're just getting deeper and deeper into debt. Always keep in mind that financial fitness does directly affect your operational readiness.

Often that great-looking stereo, TV, and furniture is worn out or replaced long before your last payment is made. Not thinking about that long-term commitment and focusing only on the enjoyment of the purchase results in the high cost of borrowing money. Then, as you get tired of the high cost over a long period of time, you end up making slow payments, late payments, and no payments, which costs you your good credit history. What's more, the resulting poor credit rating stays with you for a very long time.

Often, we don't consider all of the costs when we decide to charge it. We can all agree that using credit is convenient; unfortunately, sometimes it's too convenient. You purchase goods and services without having to carry cash. Credit enables you to purchase any item now and pay for it in the future.

Credit Cards

Credit cards can be an important tool for military personnel. For instance, when you get emergency deployed, having a credit card means you don't have to carry as much cash. As a result, you also don't have to assume all the risks of carrying cash. Furthermore, a credit card can provide purchasing power quickly under these circumstances, especially if you don't have cash that is readily accessible.

When discussing credit cards, it is necessary to address the following topics:

- Increasing debt
- All of those applications for credit cards you receive
- "Pre-Approved" sales pitches
- "Limited-time, low interest rate" deals
- Credit card collateral
- Fees for transferring credit card debt from card to card
- Ending up with two credit cards (or more)
- The high penalty fees for late payments

Increasing Debt

As stated in the introduction to this chapter, no matter what you buy with your credit card, you will pay interest on it and often other fees. Therefore, if you buy groceries on your credit card and you spend an average of $300 per month ($3,600 per year), you will be subjected to interest and fees throughout the year if you don't pay off the balance at the end of the month. This can be quite costly over time and is not in the best interest of your financial future.

Credit cards represent a rolling line of credit. You have the option to make an unlimited number of purchases until you reach your pre-approved dollar amount. That amount can range from a couple hundred dollars to several thousand dollars, depending on your credit rating. Your contract with the credit card company requires you to pay at least a portion of the balance every month. This amount is considered the minimum payment required, and is often based on a percentage of the balance. Make every effort to pay more than the minimum payments on your credit cards. Depending on the balances you have, making just the minimum payments could take decades to have completely paid off.

Don't forget to shop for the best deal on credit cards. But before you shop, be sure that you really need the card; think about what you will be using it for and if you will have the "self-control" not to overuse it. Most importantly, understand that you are expected to "pay the money back"; nothing in life worth having comes without obligations.

All of Those Applications for Credit Cards You Receive

One of the costs of having a good credit history is all of those applications you receive in the mail. Boy, they sure do look good, don't they? Be sure you read "all" of the terms of the contract; yes, ALL! You will frequently find that there are limitations or conditions. Remember, "if it sound too good to be true," it is!

"Pre-Approved" Sales Pitches

When you receive those applications in the mail, they say you are already pre-approved. Don't let these words fool you; they may not be true. You still have to fill out the information requested on the application. The card issuers will then verify your income, employment, and credit history. Then and only then you may be approved.

"Limited-Time Low Interest Rate" Deals

It is important to realize that not everyone qualifies for the rock-bottom interest rates promised in the card's promotional literature. You receive the offer, fill out the application, transfer the balance, and then find out that you didn't qualify for the great low interest rate you thought you would. The small print at the end of the offer explains this contingency. The big print "giveth" and the small print "taketh." Sometimes the grass is not always greener.

So, even though the offer might say 2.9 percent interest rate on balance transfers, you may only "qualify" for a 14.99 percent rate. As nice as all these deals seem on the surface, there's plenty to be wary about. Keep your eyes out for transaction fees when weighing different balance transfer offers. Also, avoid cards that charge large fees.

Credit Card Collateral

If you do not have a credit history or if you have had credit problems in the past, you may want to find a secured credit card. Some individuals feel they just have to have a credit card, and that feeling is supported by society. You are asked for identification while writing a check, not so with a credit card. If you are purchasing items by phone or online, frequently you can only use credit or debit cards.

So, if a secured credit card is the avenue you decide to take, you will have to pledge something of value to secure that card. For example, if you have a savings account with the bank in the amount of $500, you can then get a credit card with that amount as your credit limit. You will not be able to have access to the balance of the savings account, however; that money will assure the bank that you have the funds to pay the bill if necessary.

Using a secured credit card for a period of time will help you develop a positive credit history if you make your payments on time. Developing a positive credit history will help you get an unsecured credit card.

Fees for Transferring Credit Card Debt from Card to Card

You will find that most of the offers you receive include the option to transfer balances from one account to another. There are sometimes hidden costs associated with these transactions, however. You may think you are being rewarded with low introductory rates on any new purchases you make with the card when transferring those balances. The cost to you, however, may be more than you think it will be. Well, after the "limited time" expires, usually three months to a year, the interest will go up by several percentage points. The application should tell you what the percentage increase will be. Make sure it is not more than the card from which you transferred your balance.

In summary, as nice as these deals seem on the surface, there are several factors of which you should be aware:

- The penalties on low-rate cards can be severe; some companies charge "transaction fees" for the privilege of transferring a balance to their card. Read the small print so you are aware of "all" costs to you.
- Several cards offer low rates of 3 to 5 percent on the balance transfer charge fees when you accept their offer. Some issuers cap fees at $35 to $50 per transfer. Most companies charge these fees as soon as a balance is transferred onto a card. So, you have additional charges on your account and you haven't even used it yet.
- Once you have decided to transfer your balance from one account to another, be aware that it is important to continue to make payments on your old card while waiting for the balance transfer to take place. This could take up to four weeks. If you don't keep your payments up-to-date, it can hurt your credit history.

Ending Up With Two Credit Cards (or More)

Think about it. If you transfer the balance but you do not cut up the card from which the funds were transferred, you may be tempted to continue to use the old card. Now you have two balances to pay instead of one.

High-Penalty Fees for Late Payments

If you are late with your payments, credit cards can charge you a "late fee finance charge" and increase your debt by a predetermined interest rate that can be higher than the one you are currently paying.

Credit Cards: In the End

Of course, the best way to free up cash for the long haul is to eliminate credit card debt altogether. You'll need to continue to pay as much as you can on those cards and make every attempt to pay more than the minimum payment. Adjust those spending habits to avoid running up huge credit card balances in the future. It's all a matter of living within your means.

Remember, credit cards can be an important tool for service men and women and their families to cover such contingencies as emergency deployment and emergency family needs, such as car repairs. If you abuse them for other non-essential items, however, then they won't be there when you need them.

Chapter Five

Loans, Interest Rates & APR, and Bankruptcies

Let's face it; a debt-free existence may be unrealistic. And, in the world of personal finances, there is "good" debt, such as the car loan that provides you with needed transportation, the mortgage for the house you dream of owning, and the education loan so you can better yourself or your children. Thanks to good debt, you get to live in that great home, drive that nice car, and benefit from that education.

Think of good debt as things that appreciate or increase in value, such as homes and education. Without that mortgage, you would never be able to own a home that increases your assets; you would spend your life as a renter, increasing someone else's value. Without that car, you would not be able to get to work. And, that education offers you even more opportunities to increase your income.

Frequently, two other bonuses arise from good debt: 1) These loans typically have the lowest interest rates of all of the loans you will have. That's because of the collateral that supports them or the government that backs them; and 2) These loans typically have tax-deduction advantages.

All right, we've discussed good debt and we know that the average citizen, military or civilian, will also take on other loans. So, let's now talk about the types of loans available to you. Let's start with loans you should avoid, if possible.

Danger: Five Loans that Spell Trouble

There will always be companies ready to loan you money. It's up to you to do your research to learn about the many different types of options that are available to you. If you've gotten to the point where you're considering a loan, do your research and ask for help. Talk to the financial counselors on your installation or look for reputable financial institutions that have been in business for many years and offer financial education alternatives. (For a more in-depth look at how to protect yourself from Predatory Lending practices, see Appendix B.)

1. Payday Loans: Also known as a deferred deposit service, these are loans that are issued against your next paycheck. They are short-term, small loans that typically range from $100 to $500. To get one, you have to write a postdated check for the amount desired. For the service, you will be charged a heavy fee (frequently 10 to 20 percent of the loan balance, or 400-600% Annual Percentage Rate) for a loan lasting only a few weeks. The check cashier or payday lender holds the check until you get paid. On payday, you take cash to the lender and exchange it for your postdated check, or you allow the lender to deposit the check. If you do not show up with cash, the lender cashes the check.

    Sometimes, you can get the lender to carry the loan for another payday. If this is done, they will charge you the fee a second time and the loan rolls over. If you roll the loan over three times, you will end up paying $60 to borrow $100. How much will that $60 you just lost cost you in the next pay period? "The cycle continues." Once you start down this road, you can find your finances spiraling downward.

    Payday lending laws vary from state to state. New England states have the strictest laws, and some southern and western states have no caps on how much lenders can charge in interest and fees. The scary thing is, the national average annual percentage rate for two-week payday loans is 474 percent! Payday loans typically offer unconscionable rates and practices that negatively affect a service member's financial situation.

    Consumer organizations are pushing for a ban on expensive payday loans. Limiting the amount of interest a lender can charge or limiting the automatic rollovers would have a detrimental effect on their business and probably make payday loans unavailable to those who rely on this service.

Before you consider this option, the Federal Trade Commission recommends that you compare the loan fees, interest rates, and other costs of payday loans to other credit offers. Under the Truth in Lending Act, the cost of payday loans must be disclosed. Some financial institutions offer short-term loans that do not have these unconscionable rates and practices attached to them. Ask around in your local market for companies that offer these types of short-term lending alternatives.

2. Pawnshop Loans: There is usually a pawnshop near every military installation. Pawnshops carry terms of one to four months and are secured by a piece of property, such as a ring, a watch, or a stereo—anything that has value. Interest rates vary from state to state and range from 2 to 25 percent per loan period. Remember that if there are any fees or charges then your Annual Percentage Rate will be increased. Almost all states require pawnbrokers to allow a grace period. The collateral is sold if the interest or loan amount isn't paid off in the specified period of time. Think twice before you take your engagement ring, wedding ring, or heirloom to the shop. You might end up losing it if you can't repay the loan.

    Pawnshop loans are designed as small, short-term, quick-fix, quick-emergency cash. They are quick-help personal loan substitutes for traditional loans that the banking industry is not willing to offer because of the small amounts involved and the cost of servicing such a loan customer. The average loan is for $70 and, on average, 76 percent of borrowers eventually get their items back.

3. Title Loans: These are secured by your car's title. The lender determines how much you can borrow based on your car's value, if there is a value. If you fail to make loan payments, maybe even just one (read the small print), the lender can repossess the vehicle. Then you will have no car and you still may have to make car payments. Allowable interest rates on these types of loans vary from state to state.

4. A High Loan-to-Value Home Equity Loan: This is a loan that is secured by the equity in your home but obliges you to pay more than your equity is worth. Some home equity lenders allow you to create a loan-to-value ratio of as much as 125 percent.

    Getting a loan for more than your property is worth can be a gamble. Houses rarely sell for more than their fair market value. The interest rates on 125 percent loans are usually higher than less-risky regular home equity loans, too. And, to add insult to injury, all of the interest paid on the loan may not be tax-deductible. As you may remember from Chapter Two of this book, one of the biggest advantages of purchasing a home is the tax break you get on the interest you pay.

    To be "upside down" (owe more than it's worth) on your house and to move is really frightening. And, as you know, military personnel move frequently, sometimes with little notice. Homeowners seldom think about all the things that can happen: divorce, relocation, or being forced to move before there is any equity in the home. These are all things that can happen to a service man or woman.

5. Advance-Fee Loans: This is when a company accepts a fee in exchange for a promise to find a lender who will make a loan or issue another type of credit. These companies claim a high success rate, even with borrowers who have a tainted credit history. If you pay the fee before checking into the lender and the offer, you risk getting taken. Fees, fees, and more fees! Lenders may require consumers to pay application, appraisal, or credit report fees, but these fees are never required before the lender is identified and the application completed.

I bet you didn't know there were so many types of loans available to you that could land you with worse problems than you already have. Take the time to sit down with someone who can help you wade through all of the options you have before you choose the best path to take.

Borrowing from Family

Sometimes the only place you can go for a loan is a relative, or so you think. When people find themselves in a money crunch, a natural reaction is to turn to family for help. Parents, grandparents, and siblings are often happy to lend a financial hand via a loan.

Someone once said, "If you want to lose a friend, loan them money!" Unless handled carefully, however, family members—not just the relative advancing the cash, but others—will be resentful. There's no such thing as a family loan without emotional ties. If you don't understand that from the beginning, it will take you by surprise.

Borrowing money from parents, the most common scenario, can put you back in that familiar place you found yourself in when you were living under their roof. Mom and dad are paying the bills, and they feel entitled to tell you what to do.

Faced with the need to rely on some all-in-the-family money, how do you minimize the potential for resentment and destructive situations? Here's some advice; it won't make it perfect, but it might help:

Who are you borrowing from?

The relationship you have with the person from whom you are planning to borrow is very important. What is the worst-case scenario? If you cannot pay the money back, or if you miss payments, what will the consequences be? Let's face it; there can be so much emotion when dealing with your relatives on a normal, everyday basis, but throw in money and look out. The most important issue to consider is: are the individuals you want to borrow from good candidates? Moreover, you put people in a tough spot when they have to turn you down, thereby creating hurt feelings all around. When you ask, be prepared to handle a refusal graciously.

Get it in writing.

You must take it seriously! You have asked a family member or friend to loan you money and a letter of agreement is good. Employing the services of a lawyer is the best way to protect yourself and the lender. At the same time, it also reminds you that this is business, serious business.

Tax Laws

The amount of money you borrow is important. If your family loan is for $10,000 or more, understand that there are tax and other potential legal issues. If the person who lent you the money should die, heaven forbid, before the loan is repaid, the IRS considers unpaid loans as taxable income. You may want to consider insuring the lender's life for the amount of the loan as a way of guaranteeing repayment and avoiding tax problems.

Can You Say "Collateral?"

One way to ease the concerns of the lender (your family) is to offer specific collateral that you will give them if things don't go well. If you are forced to file bankruptcy, provided you've structured the agreement properly, your lender will have a lien on your house or your car. That will put them at the top of the list of creditors. Both you and your relative will get peace of mind from this type of arrangement. Furthermore, if you have a close enough relationship and the item is repossessed, chances are it will just be given back to you. But remember, you can only offer things you own or that are not already held in collateral by someone else (e.g., if the credit union has your car title).

Families Can't Keep Secrets

The minute you ask your mom or dad if you can borrow money, it seems everyone ends up knowing. You may think the financial deal is just between you and dad, but family secrets are hard to keep. Siblings will never let you forget it if you don't pay it back, and now they will know your financial affairs.

Get a Co-Signer

One other way that family can help without having to give you money directly from their pockets is to get them to co-sign on a loan. Sometimes lending institutions will consider lending you the money if you can find someone qualified who is willing to co-sign on the loan. The bank will accept a parent or relative's signature on the note as a guarantee. It's much more businesslike than getting a loan directly from your family member. The bank draws up all the papers. All the co-signer has to do is sign his/her name unless you fail to pay, of course. Remember, you are putting that person in a position of taking on your bills if you default.

Note: Treat friends like family when considering loans. They behave much the same way, especially those with whom you serve. There is nothing like borrowing gone wrong—it can tear your unit apart.

Personal Loans

A personal loan is another way for you to get a small amount of cash to fix a car, buy a new washing machine, or pay for your dental work. A personal loan is small, closed-ended, and unsecured. These types of loans make up one fifth (22.1 percent) of the non-mortgage installment loans on major banks' books. There is an increasing demand for these types of loans, but you will find that they are not easily accessible at all banks and credit unions. If you cannot obtain a personal loan at a bank or credit union, then ask senior leadership about other financial institutions that can help you.

When shopping for a personal loan, first decide how much money you really need. Or, better yet, decide what is the least amount needed to get you through. Consider all of the other alternatives to borrowing. If you already have a lot of debt, consider not taking on more. Examine other means of getting out of financial trouble. For instance, visit your local Consumer Credit Counseling Service to see how they can help you.

Once you determine that you do need to take on a loan and you start shopping, you will find that terms vary considerably. Check with your bank, credit union, or other financial institution and talk about what rates you can expect to see.

Here is a quick checklist to use when considering a personal loan:

- Look at the total cost of the credit, remembering that lower monthly payments are not always better. There may be hidden costs, so look at all associated fees. The interest rate may also be higher and the length of the loan may be longer.

- Ask questions; have the person helping you itemize and explain all of the charges. Ask about anything you don't understand.
- Walk out if what you see on the contract is different from what the lending agent tells you. What you are told by the agent is meaningless once you sign on the dotted line. The only thing that counts is what is in writing.
- With loans "bigger is not always better." You will find that the loan officer will suggest that you borrow more than you need. Consider what your true needs are before taking out a larger loan and what you can handle financially. Doing so will also help you with your budgeting.
- One of the most important things to consider is the institution that you are borrowing from. Have they been in business for a long time? Do they understand the military? Do they offer financial education to customers? These are some of the questions you should ask of a company that you are considering getting a loan from. The key to obtaining financial freedom is your ability to do your homework and understand as much as possible about the process.

Breaking the Debt Cycle: Pay Down Your Unproductive Loans First

So, you're tired of all the debt you are carrying and how it has put "handcuffs" on you and your family. You'd like to pay off or pay down your debt, but where do you start?

In the world of personal finances there are productive and unproductive loans. Productive loans are loans such as car, house, and education loans. These are called productive loans for two reasons: one, because it's unlikely that you could come up with the full cash amount to buy the items covered; and two, because you get tax advantages with these loans. Unproductive loans are the loans you want to get rid of first. These loans typically have high annual percentage rates and are the kind you wish you never took in the first place (e.g., to fix the car because you didn't have an emergency fund saved or to consolidate debts that became too much for you to handle).

Understanding the difference between productive and unproductive debt enables you to appropriately reduce your debt level, which in turn improves your long-term financial situation.

Productive Loans

People often refer to their mortgage as the albatross around their neck, citing the large balance and the many years of mortgage payments stretching out ahead of them. Owing a lot of dollars for a lot of years can seem overwhelming. For the typical debt-laden consumer, however, mortgage debt is not the burden you think it is.

Mortgage debt is typically low-cost debt and one whose cost is further reduced by the tax-deductibility of the mortgage interest. The tax deduction is usually big enough to offset taxes incurred from other income, thus reducing the true cost of the mortgage for many homeowners.

Furthermore, while many consider the monthly mortgage payment as debt service, it can really be viewed as dollar-cost averaging into an appreciating asset. The monthly mortgage payment becomes more of an investment and less of a debt service as time passes. The more years into the loan, the more each payment builds equity and the less interest is paid. The steady appreciation of property values is also capable of minimizing, and sometimes offsetting entirely, the cost of financing the loan. If the only debt a borrower has outstanding is this low-cost, so-called productive debt, there is no hurry to pay it off.

Unproductive Loans

The true hazard to financial security is higher-rate loans, such as credit card purchases, cash advances, or payday loans. These debts eat away at your secure financial future. This is where your past spending habits come back to haunt you. These loans give you none of the great benefits, such as tax-deductibility or the appreciation of value of an asset, which productive loans do. Whenever you can, pay those loans down first.

The best strategy is to pay down your loans in order of cost, from the highest percentage rate to the lowest. And remember, it is not the fact that you have a loan that may threaten your financial security. More importantly, it is the type of loan.

Interest Rates, APR, and Other Important Terms

Once you decide that you need to look into credit or a loan, the next question you need to ask is: what are the terms and conditions of the credit? For example, what is the interest rate you will pay?

What follows are the definitions of interest rate, APR, fees, grace period, and balance computation methods, all of which are important to you when deciding which loan or credit you should get.

Interest Rate

Interest is money paid for the use of borrowed money. This concept affects how much money you will pay for borrowing money. Interest rates can be fixed or variable. A "fixed" rate means you will pay the same rate throughout the life of the loan. A "variable" rate, on the other hand, means that the rate will vary up or down. This interest rate is typically tied to the national "prime" interest rate. The written terms of the loan or credit card will indicate when and how often the interest rate can change. The interest rate assigned to your credit varies with the lender, your current debt, your credit history, and the length of time of the loan. (To learn about sub-prime vs. prime lending and how it affects your interest rate, see Appendix A.)

Annual Percentage Rate (APR)

APR reflects the interest rate plus any fees or charges you will be charged and will be expressed as a rate of interest. Therefore, the APR contains all credit costs. The APR is intended to make it easier for borrowers to compare the cost of credit from one lender to another. In other words, it allows borrowers to compare "apples to apples" as opposed to "apples to pears."

For example, two lenders may say that their interest rates are the same: 10 percent. However, the one lender's fees may be more per year than the other lender's fees. This difference would show up in the APR. Therefore, the one lender's APR may be 10.40 percent while the other lender's APR may be 10.15 percent. All lending institutions are required to give you their APR.

Note: Both interest rates and APRs shown on applications are sometimes promotional. Read the disclosure—you may find that after a period of time, the promotional APR will expire and then it goes up. It is very important to understand the difference between Interest Rate and Annual Percentage Rate.

Fees

What are fees? Fees add up and can be very expensive. They include:
- Annual fees (sometimes these will be waived if you have good credit);
- Late fees (these are typically a fixed dollar amount that is charged no matter how late—the cost of procrastination could be as much as $30);
- Late Charges (these are usually a percentage of the balance owed on the debt and are often based on how late you are);
- Fees if you go over the limit (these are usually associated with credit cards);
- Loan Origination Fees; and
- Finally, you may even be charged for closing the account.

Grace Period

A grace period is the time (days) you have to pay your balance before the credit card company starts charging you interest or late fees depending on the type of transaction.

Balance Computation Methods

The balance computation calculation will determine how your interest is figured. The most common method is average daily balance. Be aware that there are other methods that will cost you more over the long run.

I'll bet you didn't think there was so much to think about when looking into loans, credit card interest rates, and APRs. The biggest thing to consider is whether you can afford to apply for that loan. Our world today makes accumulating debts as easy as filling in the forms. However, the potential consequences are too horrible to think about.

Bankruptcy

Since lenders make it very easy to accumulate debt, chances are you will find yourself in over your head in debt at some point in your life. At this point, you might be asking yourself: what is bankruptcy and am I a candidate?

Bankruptcy is a legal remedy and, as such, only an attorney can properly advise you on the process. My experience has been that the decision is based partially on facts, partially on emotions, and partially on a person's view of his/her future.

As in so much of life, there are no hard and fast rules to determine if you are a candidate for bankruptcy. Everyone's financial/emotional/future situation is different. One person with $25,000 in debts can sleep at night and doesn't worry. A different person with that same amount of debt stays awake at night and worries all of the time. The situation affects their operational readiness. Those individuals in such a situation may feel that they have no other choice but to declare bankruptcy. Others may see great future opportunities for themselves and find ways to clear the debts, certainly ways to clear their "past due" situations.

What is most important to keep in mind is that bankruptcy should be used with caution and with a full understanding of the consequences. I think of it in the same vein as handling explosives. It may be the right thing to use for the job you are doing but it comes at a potentially high cost: consequences! Always consult your attorney or other financial professional before making decisions regarding bankruptcy.

Looking at the three points briefly, there are financial, emotional, and future implications to consider.

1. First, do the math on how much you owe, what the payments are and what income you can devote to the payments, then decide whether or not you can free up or get more/enough income. Increasing your income may be difficult in the service, especially within a short period of time.

2. Second, rate your emotional position. Can you stand being in debt any longer? Are the creditor calls getting to you? Can you sleep at night? Are you fighting with your spouse?

    As military personnel, bankruptcy is a high risk to your position. Not only can it affect your operational readiness, which in turn affects your safety and the safety of your unit, but it can also affect the success of your mission. Furthermore, has your commanding officer been informed about your debt? Are you in danger of losing your security clearance?

3. Third, assess your future prospects and the consequences of a bankruptcy. Finally, see an attorney or financial professional to explore any other ways out of the situation. Look at it as a battle: surrendering is a last resort!

Bankruptcy can affect your promote-ability, new job applications, renting a new apartment, insurance, and your ability to make major purchases. Do you see your life as on an upward trend or a downward slide? What are your goals for the next two to ten years?

There are many alternatives to bankruptcy, including settling your debts for less than what is owed. Credit counseling is also available at your installation. These options are all worth checking out before committing to bringing in the big guns!

Solving problems through the courts rarely produces a satisfying result. So if you go ahead, expect to get rid of your debts but don't expect to walk away feeling like a winner. Also, make sure to do your homework and to seek professional advice.

Here are 20 instances that could indicate your balances are getting the better of you and that credit counseling might help:

1. Your credit card balances are increasing, but you have no way to increase your income.

2. You are only paying the minimum amounts required on your accounts, or maybe even less than the minimums. Furthermore, the amount of finance charges being added to your balance almost equals what you are paying each month.

3. You're juggling bills. You pay one company with credit from another company.

4. You have two or more active credit cards opened.

5. You have come close to maximizing all of your credit cards.

6. You are charging more each month than you are paying.

7. You are working overtime to keep up with your credit card payments.

8. You don't keep track of what you owe; you adopt the attitude of "ignorance is bliss."

9. Your creditors are calling your Commanding Officer, reporting delinquent bill payments.

10. You are using your credit card to buy necessities like food or gasoline and leisure items like CDs and DVDs.

11. You use your credit card because you have no money to make your purchases.

12. You "rob Peter to pay Paul," Peter doesn't get paid, and then you charge it.

13. You are hiding the true cost of your purchases from your spouse.

14. You're playing the card game by signing up for every credit card that sends you an unsolicited offer.

15. Your spouse just lost her/his job or is fearful that s/he will. S/he is also concerned about how you will pay all the bills.

16. You put your unopened bill envelopes in the drawer.

17. With all the payments you make each month on credit card debt, you have no extra cash for savings and investments.

18. You do not cut up your card after you pay off the balance.

19. You have no emergency fund and no light at the end of the tunnel.

20. You cannot get any additional credit because your credit report is negative.

Look for a pattern. There's no magic number of indicators to determine if you have a credit problem. Even if you see yourself in several of these above instances, you still might be able to deal with your credit crunch on your own.

If you spot a trend, however, beware. For example, don't panic if you occasionally shop surreptitiously, not letting your spouse in on your splurge. Anybody might do this on occasion. If it's becoming routine, however, you probably have a problem.

Similarly, paying only the "minimum payment required" once in a while could be acceptable. If it's more than an isolated money management misstep, however, you could be headed for trouble. If you see some of these warning signs, you need to take a serious look and find out why. Perhaps it's something temporary, like you're between jobs. If it's becoming a bad pattern, however, you need to be honest. Admitting you have a problem will go at least halfway toward solving it.

If you find that your debts are getting out of hand, the last thing you want to do is ignore them. Hiding your head in the sand will not make the bills go away. The longer you let them go, the worse it gets. Sitting down to discuss things with your lenders is the responsible thing to do. Most of your lenders would rather know there is a problem and help you than have you be unresponsive to their calls. If you talk with them, they at least know you will try to solve the problem. Also talk to your financial institution to see if they have any financial education programs to help you better understand your situation.

If you neglect your bills and do not talk with your creditors, they will turn your debt over to bill collectors. If your case is turned over to creditors, you do have rights. You have a right to receive written notice of to whom and what you owe as well as what you can do if you wish to dispute a bill.

Don't wait too long; it's far easier on families to seek help sooner rather than later. If you do not feel you owe the debt, you can send a letter within 30 days notifying the party that you question the bill. They then have to send you proof of the bill and they cannot call you until they do. Moreover, they cannot be abusive, unfair, or deceitful.

Chapter Six

Creating a Stable Future

You love your military job and you take pride in serving your country. As a result, you want to keep this job. You want to be able to financially take care of yourself and your family, and you want financial stability for your future.

If you haven't gotten yourself into credit problems yet, start with saying NO; just say no to all of those things you don't have to have! You have already read all of the reasons why you should keep from borrowing and using credit. Stick with your financial goals and your budget.

For some of you, unfortunately, you may feel like the information in this book came too late. You already have credit issues and now you need information on how to dig yourself out of your debt.

Where do you go from here? You're in the military. You need a plan, a process to ensure your mission's success. And in this case, your mission is to get your financial stuff together!

Get Your Credit Report

First, you want to order your credit report and check out your "creditworthiness." Anyone who has used credit in the past has a "credit record," a history of using credit and a log of how you pay or do not pay your bills. All of that activity becomes a "permanent" record, for at least seven years. Your credit history is tracked through several reporting agencies. The most prominent of these are:

Equifax
P.O. Box 740241
Atlanta, GA 30374
www.equifax.com

Experian
PO Box 2104
Allen, TX 75013
www.experian.com

TransUnion
Post Office Box 2000
Chester, PA 19022
www.transunion.com

These companies track an individual's credit usage, payment histories, and other factors, all of which are taken into account when determining a person's creditworthiness. You have a right to receive a copy of your report for a small fee, and there is also new legislation enacted stating that each person is entitled to one free credit report per year.

Your credit history will list personal information, which will include: credit card information such as what credit cards you have opened and whether or not they maintain balances; mortgage and other debt balances; and your payment history. It will also include all of the inquiries, or the names of creditors and other "authorized" parties who have requested and received your credit report.

Your potential lender evaluates all of this information. A lender will also look at your income, savings, liquid assets, job security, and credit limits as a means of ensuring the loan is appropriate for your income and financial stability. You will be charged a higher interest rate or receive a lower credit limit based on the information they see.

Be aware that your credit history also contains "public record" information. This includes bankruptcies, foreclosures (your mortgage lender takes back your property for lack of payment), collection accounts (an account that has been referred to a collection agency), tax liens (a claim against property or assets by a tax authority for unpaid taxes), civil judgments, and late child support payments.

Consider having your credit report examined by a Certified Credit Report Reviewer to help you understand what your credit report means and how you can improve it. Maintaining your credit rating is a key to your financial success.

Consumer Credit Counseling Services

If you need to talk with someone who can help you with your credit problems, you may choose to use a credit counseling agency. Okay, read this carefully! There are basically two kinds of credit counseling services: 1) those that are trustworthy and do all that they can for you for reasonable fees or no fees; and 2) those that make promises they frequently cannot keep and that attempt to get rich off your terrible situation through fees and the types of payment arrangements they make. For the sake of further discussion, we will label these as "Trustworthy" and "Avoid At All Costs" credit counseling agencies.

Trustworthy Agencies

If you choose to use credit counseling, here are some questions that are recommended by the National Foundation for Consumer Credit:
- Is this agency a nonprofit organization?
- How much will their services cost?
- Are their services confidential?
- Will they devise a plan that is tailored to fit your needs?
- Are their counselors certified?
- Will your funds be protected?
- Is the agency accredited?

Make sure that the debt management or credit counseling firm answers all of your questions and that you have a firm understanding of how the process works. Most importantly, find out what it will cost you. If you do not get the answers to your questions or you do not understand what's going on, don't sign up with that company.

Be cool under fire. This is not the time to panic and make a decision that costs you more money and delays in getting your problems fixed. View this as a military "situation." Meet with the agency's personnel, gather information, evaluate that information, and then make a decision that is best for you. No intimidation, no fear!

The Consumer Credit Counseling Services (CCCS) is a national organization that helps people with credit problems. They aren't miracle workers, but frequently they make a dramatic difference; it depends on how long you put off calling them. But no matter how "lost" the situation seems, always visit them to see what they can do.

Most debt counseling agencies are nonprofit organizations that get much of their financial support from the credit card industry. They offer numerous services, including debt-management plans. When you enroll in one of these debt-management plans, you write one check a month to the agency and the agency pays your creditors for you. In a typical debt management program, a card issuer will charge lower interest rates, will eliminate late fees, and will lower monthly payments. In addition, you will get fewer calls and letters from bill collectors. Debt counseling agencies obtain their operating money by receiving a percentage back from client's payments to each creditor.

There are plenty of reputable credit counseling agencies that assist people with all kinds of money problems. They also charge low fees for debt management programs and other services. They include members of the AICCCA and the National Foundation of Credit Counseling, the oldest network of nonprofit counseling agencies. The AICCCA's debt management fee limit for their enrollment is $75.00 and monthly service fees run no higher than $50.00. Many other member agencies' fees fall well below these numbers.

These organizations usually only handle "secured credit" obligations but will occasionally take on some "unsecured" credit, such as credit card companies. This is how it works. They will mediate a repayment schedule for you based on a 3–5 year time frame. Be aware that this service can cost you money. Even though they do reduce your required monthly payment, they may not reduce their finance charges. What does this mean? It means a 48- or 60-month contract will be increased by many months and the total finance charge may be much higher than the original contract terms.

These organizations may also add additional finance charges for the increased term.

Avoid-At-All-Costs Agencies

If you trust the wrong company, getting help could be downright dangerous to your wallet and your credit rating. A lot of credit counseling and debt consolidation companies are looking to make a quick buck by preying on stressed-out, financially vulnerable consumers. Some companies are guilty of merely shoddy service and sky-high fees. Others are out-and-out scams.

Why are these fly-by-night companies opening outside every base in the United States? As a nation, we are wrestling with $723 billion in credit card debt. Toss in an economy that is slow and it comes as no surprise why so many of these individuals are turning to these types of companies for help.

Be aware that some agencies pocket the first month of credit payments for themselves. So, right off the bat, you're a month behind. The result? Your credit accounts get slammed with late fees and penalty interest rates. Instead of being current, you're a month behind. Most consumers are not aware of how some of these agencies work. If it's in the fine print, it's the consumer's responsibility to read it. Read everything!

With some of these arrangements, you might be surprised that in order to stay current on your debt, you will have to pay your monthly credit bills on your own. That's on top of the hefty upfront fee you pay the agency. That means you pay two months' worth of creditor payments in a single month. That might prove impossible for someone who is already having trouble paying his or her debts in the first place.

By employing the services of some of these agencies, your financial situation can continue to get worse. Let's say you are paying minimum payments on your Sears or MasterCard that, on its own, will take you at least ten years to pay off; then, throw in the renegotiated payment and you could end up paying off your mortgage before you get your credit card paid off.

Choose wisely. Complaints against debt consolidation companies are at an all-time high according to the Council of Better Business Bureaus.

Other Things to Consider When Choosing a Credit Counseling Agency:

- Cold Calls—Don't use a company that solicits you either over the phone or by spam e-mails. When seeking a trustworthy agency, try to:
  - Ask a family member or friend to get a referral. It is always better to use an agency that has been referred by a happy client.
  - Do your own research; read the agreement carefully. A smart consumer will know what s/he is getting into.
  - Check with the Better Business Bureau to determine if the agency you are choosing to work with has a satisfactory rating or if any complaints against it have been successfully resolved.
- Large Upfront Fees—The fees you pay should not be more than $50.00 to establish a debt management plan or $35.00 each month to maintain your plan.
- Convenience counseling—Once you decide on a company, the counselor should meet you in person, over the phone, or over the Internet for at lease one hour to determine the best program for your situation, rather than pushing the quickest solution for them.
- High-pressure sales pitch—These companies are supposed to be there as a service to you. A sales pitch should not be used. Instead, you should receive encouragement and support from the person you are talking to.
- Debt-elimination—If a company claims that they can eliminate your debt and that you do not have to make any payments without repercussions, they are being untruthful. Such agencies will claim that the debt you have incurred using credit cards is not legal debt. They will base this claim on information from Title 15 of the United States Code—Section 1692, the Fair Debt Collections Practices Act; Section 1601, the Fair Credit Billing Act; and the Uniform Commercial Code, Section 203. If there is a law that states it is illegal for credit card companies to extend you credit, why are there billions of credit cards in circulation? Furthermore, don't you think this fact would have come to the attention of lawmakers who, by now, would have enforced this law?

Face the facts: you accumulated the debt to purchase stereos, furniture, CDs, automobiles, clothing, and other possessions you wanted. The time has now come when you have to pay for what you bought. If you have overextended yourself and are having trouble making the payments, it does not mean that you do not owe the money. If you are having trouble, legitimate help is available to assist you in repaying your debt, but not to totally eliminate it.

Now, think about the rest of your debt. The problem is not only the debt we discussed. Usually when you have problems with your credit card debt, you will also have trouble paying your everyday expenses. What's more, these are the bills you cannot negotiate down. The problem lies in how you manage your money in the first place. Is CCCS the solution or is the solution for you to learn how to manage your income and pay all of your bills and debt?

One additional item that is obvious is that in order to solve your credit and spending problems, you will need to stop spending beyond your means (continuing to charge your purchases). That is the only way you will ever get out of debt. If you are able to do this now, then next year will be a very good year indeed.

Identity Theft

The only thing worse than running up those credit cards, taking out those loans, and getting yourself into terrible money trouble is someone else stealing your identity and running up bills in your name. With your name and Social Security number, your birthday, and other personal information such as credit card numbers, insurance information, and bank account numbers, such thieves will have the ability to establish new credit, to run up debt, or to take over existing accounts. This will not only ruin your credit but it could leave you with bills you didn't run up. It will likely also cause many headaches in the process.

Protecting your personal information is vital. Did you know that many businesses share or sell your information without knowing how it will be used? Your bank's or insurance companies' "Privacy Statement" can stop such organizations from selling your name and personal information. When shopping online or by catalog, you should instruct these vendors not to sell your information to other vendors. A good indication that your information is being sold is those six additional catalogs you receive in the mail right after you place that order.

According to a report from the Federal Trade Commission, identity theft again tops the list of consumer complaints. Identity thieves rob more than 500,000 Americans every year. Credit can be damaged and fixing it can cost you hundreds of dollars and take up hundreds of hours of your time. The following steps will help you reduce your risk of identity theft.

Fifteen Tips to Avoid Identity Theft

1. The key to your personal information is your Social Security number. As such, it is the prime target of criminals. Guard it well.
2. Monitor your credit report annually since it will contain all of your personal information, such as your Social Security number, your current and prior employers, a listing of all your open and closed account numbers, and your overall credit score. After applying for a loan, a credit card, a rental, or anything else that requires a credit report, request that your Social Security number on the application be completely destroyed and that your original credit report either be shredded before your eyes or returned to you once a decision has been made. A lender or rental manager needs to retain only your name and credit score to justify a decision.
3. Keep all receipts, statements, and credit card numbers in a safe place and shred them when you are ready to dispose of them. Shred all old bank and credit statements and any "junk mail" credit card offers before trashing them.
4. Remove your name from the marketing lists of the three credit reporting bureaus to reduce the number of pre-approved credit offers you receive.
5. Add your name to the name deletion lists of the Direct Marketing Association's Mail Preference Service and the Telephone Preference Service used by banks and other marketers.

6. Do not carry extra credit cards or other important identity documents, except when needed.

7. Place the contents of your wallet on a photocopy machine. Copy both sides of your license and credit cards so you have all the account number expiration dates and phone numbers if your wallet or purse is stolen. Close unused accounts, immediately close bank accounts, and establish new ones if your wallet is stolen.

8. Do not mail bill payments and checks from home. They can be stolen from your mailbox and washed clean in chemicals. Take them to the post office instead.

9. Never print your Social Security number on your checks.

10. Keep the Social Security Earnings and Benefits statements sent to you once a year around your birthday and check them for fraud.

11. Examine the charges on your credit card statements before paying them.

12. Cancel unused credit card accounts.

13. Never give your credit card number or personal information over the phone, unless you have initiated the call and trust that business.

14. Subscribe to a credit report monitoring service that will notify you whenever someone applies for credit in your name.

15. Review your credit card statements, utility bills, and bank statements for accuracy or for any unusual activity. Immediately report anything you feel is incorrect.

Identity theft is a white-collar crime and most police departments are not equipped with the tools necessary to investigate each case. The bad news is that these cases are not usually solved. In fact, prosecution occurs less than 10 percent of the time. Most times, these criminals are not working alone. As a group, they steal several different identities at a time and leave behind an untraceable trail.

If this happens to you, the result will be a ruined credit history and a lot of time trying to get your finances in order. The average cost of identity theft tops $18,000 and does not include cases where the thief retains a job and where employers incur additional costs.

The 10 Things Anyone Can Find Out About You:

1. Your current and previous address (from the US Postal Service and credit bureaus)
2. Any criminal convictions (from court records)
3. Whether you have a professional license (from licensing agencies)
4. Whether you have filed lawsuits or been a defendant in a lawsuit (from court records)
5. If you've had speeding tickets, drunken driving convictions, or other black marks on your driving record (from the drivers' license bureau)
6. What cars, trucks, boats, and planes you own (from state motor vehicle records)
7. Whether you have filed for bankruptcy or had liens placed against your property (from court records)
8. What you have pledged as collateral for bank loans (from Universal Commercial Code filings, usually in county recorders' offices)
9. What pieces of real estate you own and how much you paid for them (from county tax records)
10. Whether there's a warrant out for your arrest (from court records and police agencies)

Don't be a victim of identity theft. Take the necessary precautions to protect yourself from fraud and corruption.

Chapter Seven

How to Invest

In the previous chapters, we discussed budgeting, purchasing major items, dealing with major events, credit, and all areas related to credit counseling, management, and consolidation. In this chapter, we will discuss investment strategies, specifically understanding the investment options available to you and the benefits of investing for your short-, intermediate- and long-term financial goals.

Money investment strategies are similar to your military career strategies; you have short-term and long-term strategies. Instead of deciding where you will invest your money, achievement of your military career goals consists of where you will invest your time. In the military, strategies for achieving your short-term career goals can consist of spending time in performing your current job with top-notch skills, being a strong team player, behaving in a manner that demonstrates respect to your chain of command, and preparing for your next promotion. Long-term career strategies can include an investment of time in researching who has reached the top positions, enlisted or officer, and how s/he achieved that goal (e.g., types and locations of duty held, personality types, and MOS, Rating, or Billets held). Always consult the appropriate legal and financial professionals regarding your individual investment decisions.

A good way to think about investing is:
- Career = Investment of Time Strategies
- Future Finances = Investment of Money Strategies

As with your military career strategies, the sooner you evaluate your finances, set goals for them, and work toward them, the better off you will be. You will be better off for two reasons:
- You will have money tucked away in an investment that can be used for your future; and

- You will form a habit of always looking for more money to grow your investment.

Remember that how we behave with our money is a result of our money habits. Create good money habits just like you have created good military habits (e.g., being on time, being "pressed," and being respectful).

Beyond your short-term saving, the methods used in long-term saving are called investing or investments. Investing over the long term is sometimes called financial planning. You might think that you need to have extra money if you want to have a financial plan. That assumption, however, is untrue; rather, you need the "plan" to be set in place so that when you have money left over in your budget, that additional money will already be targeted for the investment of your choice.

Don't Delay

Individuals often delay investing for a number of reasons. If you are one of these people, you may feel that:

- You do not have enough money to invest.
- You do not understand the options that may be available to you.
- You are too young to worry about investing.
- Investing is too risky.
- You do not know what choices are available to you.
- You do not have enough time to get the plan together.
- You do not need to worry about it; the military will take care of you.

These are all excuses, and you know how far excuses will get you in the service.

Getting Started

Note that inflation works against your savings and investments. When considering how much money you will need to reach your financial goals, you will need to factor in the impact of inflation on the cost of living. If you have an inflation factor of 3.5 percent, the money you spend today for your living expenses will double in 20 years. That means that if you are living on an income of $20,000 today and you have 40 years until you are planning to retire, you will need $80,000 for the same living expenses when you retire. The impact of inflation will also affect any long-term financial goals you may have, such as college planning for your newborn child.

To get started, you should determine your investment goals. Think of them in three different time frames: short-, intermediate-, and long-term. You should also recognize that the investment products you choose have different potentials for growth and for risk of loss; typically, if they have a potential for a high percentage rate of earnings, they also have a higher potential for loss. To increase the possibility of success, you need to educate yourself. Thoroughly investigate the options and sources of assistance available to you. Armed with these resources, you will be able to implement a successful plan.

Let's face facts. For a while there, investing was so easy that anyone could make money in the stock market. And everyone bragged about how much money they had made. Unfortunately, reality reared its ugly head and all those high-flying portfolios with their paper profits came crashing back to earth. That's when a lot of people who thought that getting rich in the market was easy discovered that ignorance wasn't simply bliss; it was also hazardous to their wealth. Think about it. If putting together a profitable portfolio were that easy, why isn't everybody rich already?

Still, despite the occasional downturn of the market, people do build fortunes in the stock market. Over the long haul, investors with a sound strategy make money during the good times and hold onto their cash through the hard times. The key lies in holding onto your investment no matter what. Only if you have done your homework and reevaluated your sound strategy, goals, and objective every year will you achieve financial growth. The question, of course, is: which sound strategy should I choose?

Strategies

As it turns out, there are several solid strategies you can employ, and experts disagree over which is best. (It's sort of like strategies for getting in shape or for preparing for a military promotion test; the experts all have different strategies or ways of going about it.) Most investment experts, however, do agree that what's most important is having a strategy and sticking with it through all markets, both "bull" and "bear."

To help you make a choice, we've defined the five most popular investment strategies so you can see how they compare. Remember as you read about these different strategies that they all deal with how to take your assets (money) and convert/put them into various investment categories called stocks, bonds/debt securities, mutual funds, and individual investment accounts.

Buy and Hold

This is the most conservative way to invest, but it may also be the most reliable and safe. Investors simply choose either quality stable/blue chip stocks or mutual funds and hold them for many years.

Long-term investors don't worry about market fluctuations because they figure that their stocks will have time to recover from a down market. No more looking at the stock ticker every 15 minutes. Just sit back, relax, and wait for your rewards. You will also save a bundle on broker commissions because you're not paying for frequent transactions.

The catch is that choosing the right time to sell your investments can be tricky. You can counter this problem somewhat by knowing in advance when you'll need the money; this tactic involves planning.

Asset Allocation

This is a means of balancing your investment portfolio, with "Asset" being your money and "Allocation" meaning to divide or split your money into different investments. Simply stated, it means to divide or split your money among stocks, bonds, mutual funds, cash, and other kinds of security investments. Dividing or splitting is the key decision that determines investment success. Using this method allows you to stop worrying about your ability to choose the right stocks, bonds, or mutual funds. This process may include one or all of the following processes:

- Strategic Asset Allocation: Uses historical information in an attempt to understand how the asset has performed in the past and is likely to perform over long periods of time. With this process, the goal is not to try to "beat" the market, but to establish a long-term investment strategy using a core mix of assets.

- Tactical Asset Allocation: Uses periodic assumptions regarding the current performance and characteristics of the asset and/or the economy. This process involves "mid-course" changes based on what is happening to improve the potential of your investments.
- Dynamic Asset Allocation: This is a very important strategy since it is used when there is a change in the investor's (your) circumstances. These changes may affect goals, objectives, and/or risk tolerance. Getting married, having children, moving, getting divorced, and being deployed are all examples of why your investment tactics might need to be changed.

For example, you could create a global equity portfolio made up of 80 percent U.S. companies and 20 percent international stocks. You might then further subdivide that portfolio between small and large companies, both here and abroad.

These methods minimize your risk, but they also lessen the chance that you'll strike it rich. That's because you're not heavily invested in one area. In other words, you won't strike out, but you're also not likely to hit a home run either. Still, many financial planners prefer the safety of having steady, though unspectacular returns.

Diversification

Having a diversified portfolio and holding on to it for long periods of time is a successful strategy that many financial advisors use. Depending on the array of stocks that you choose, the results will be different. Over five-year periods, however, they'll almost always be positive and certainly will be over 10- and 20-year periods. You can diversify your investments in three ways:

1. Diversify among various investment alternatives (stocks, bonds, mutual funds).
2. Diversify within a particular type of investment by investing in several different companies (e.g., all utility, healthcare, transportation companies).

3. Diversify in bonds or other fixed income investments according to maturity dates.

Dollar-Cost Averaging

This is one of the most reliable and simple investment plans. If you have a 401(k) plan that automatically withdraws from your paycheck, you're dollar-cost averaging. To employ this strategy on your own, put a set amount into a mutual fund every month.

The neat thing about this system is that when the market is down, you are buying more shares of stock (or funds) at a lower price. When the market is going up, you buy fewer shares at a higher price. You don't worry about what the market is doing; you just keep buying regularly, automatically averaging your cost as you go.

If you have a large sum of money to invest, such as a deployment bonus or an inheritance, you could invest it all at once or you could open a Money Market account and have specific amounts invested every month.

You can dollar-cost average by having money automatically withdrawn from a bank account, thereby avoiding the need for a minimum deposit. Some mutual fund companies will waive the required minimum deposit if you agree to make automatic deposits each month. This strategy will help you sleep at night and accomplishes several things:

- Helps you practice discipline and have a plan to save and invest regularly.
- Provides you with the opportunity to buy more shares of your investment at a lower price when the market is down.
- Gives you an average cost per share that is below transaction price.

Emotional Investing

You may have a handle on your investments, but do you have a handle on your emotions? Managing emotions is more important because when your emotions run wild, you make decisions that will more than likely damage your financial success. As a human being, you can be your own worst enemy. You can create investment risks through your fear, greed, and lack of knowledge. When investing, you will need to manage your emotions with rational strategies.

Managing Risk

Investing is the process of buying an asset and hoping that it will increase in value over time. Your risk tolerance will be the measure of where you invest your money. Is risk really what we think it is? The amount of risk tolerance varies from person to person.

Unfortunately, you cannot avoid risk. If you invest your "long-term" money into low interest rate performers, such as a Money Market account, CDs, and/or savings accounts, the risk you face is that your money will not grow enough to outperform the cost of taxes and inflation. In other words, you have money set aside but after taxes and inflation, it is worth less than the original amount you put in. On the other hand, if you invest your "short-term" money into stocks, long-term bonds or mutual funds, you risk the loss of funds if you need your money (have to cash out or sell) while the market is on a downtrend. The same investment could be low-risk or high-risk, depending on your time frame.

One of the major problems you will encounter in risk management is how you define what risk is. When you discuss risk as related to investing, it is most likely used as a synonym for volatility. In other words, how quickly can the investment go up or down?

To begin the investment process, ask yourself these questions:
- Is inflation a major influence on the outcome of your investments?
- Can you dollar-cost average?
- How can you tell what the right investment is for you?
- Should you invest in stocks?
- Should you invest in bonds?
- Are mutual funds right for you to invest in?

We have discussed investment strategies. Now let's discuss the different investment categories into which you put your assets/money: stocks, bonds/debt securities, mutual funds, and individual investment accounts.

Stocks

Stocks represent segments of ownership in a corporation. When you purchase stock you "own" part of the company in which you invest. The value of your stock initially depends on the amount of shares the company has issued for sale. If at the time of initial offering of stock the company's worth is $2,000,000 and it issues 200,000 shares of stock, each share is worth $10.00 (worth divided by number of shares). As the owner or stockholder, you share in the profits or losses of the company and you can vote on decisions about how the company is managed.

After the initial offering, the value of the stock varies with the market demand for the stock, which can fluctuate depending on how the company or the economy as a whole performs.

Common Stock is securities representing the equity ownership in a corporation, usually with voting rights, and provides the shareholder with a share of the company's earnings through dividends or capital appreciation. These earnings will vary based on the company's performance.

Preferred Stock provides a dividend that is paid before any dividends are paid to holders of common stock. Preferred stock owners usually do not have voting rights and they represent partial ownership in the company.

- Blue Chip Stock comes from large corporations with a steady growth rate and dividend payments, like General Electric, IBM, and Procter & Gamble.
- Small Cap Stocks are stocks in companies that present more risk and smaller market capitalization (number of outstanding shares times the price per share) of $250 million to $1 billion.
- Mid Cap Stocks are stocks in companies with a market capitalization of $1.5 billion to $5 billion.
- Large Cap Stocks are stocks in companies with a market capitalization of over $5 billion.

The smaller the company, the higher the risk of loss of principal on the money you invested.

When purchasing stocks follow these seven strategies:

- Buy discriminatingly.

- Research industries.
- Diversify your portfolio.
- Buy low/sell high.
- Watch market trends.
- Buy for value.
- Look for dividend payments.

Bonds/Debt Securities

Bonds are debt obligations of a publicly owned company or governmental agency. In other words, if such organizations need money, they can sell bonds to you to help raise the necessary funds and then promise to pay you back that money with interest. You, along with all of the others buying the bonds, act in a lending manner that is similar to a bank.

Many types of debt securities can be used for the short-, intermediate-, and long-term goals we have discussed throughout this book. Bonds do not reflect ownership but are obligations to repay the loan you have made over some period of time, with a set interest payment to you. Bonds are sold with a "face value" and a stated rate of return or interest rate.

The value of the bond may change over the length of the ownership term, based on how much people want to pay for that bond. Each of the following bonds has a current market price and a set interest rate.

- Municipal bonds are those bonds that are issued by the state or local government to finance public works projects or services. The advantage of municipal bonds is that they are not taxed by the federal government and, in some cases, may not be taxed by the state.
- Junk bonds are highly speculative and risky investments. Only those individuals who can tolerate great risks of their money should purchase these types of bonds. Junk bonds have the potential for big growth but they also have the risk for a big loss of principal.
- Savings Bonds and Certificates of Deposit can be used for both short-term savings and long-term investments with set interest payments. These investments are less risky since they are insured

by a governmental agency. A regular savings account provides easy access to your funds, but pays a lower rate of return. A Certificate of Deposit, on the other hand, pays a higher return but obligates you to keep your money in the account for a specific period of time. This time commitment can range anywhere from one month to several years. Savings bonds are sold by the United States Government and are another longer-term investment option.

In uncertain times it is wise to maintain some portion of your financial portfolio in fixed income investments (those with guaranteed percentage earnings). Although they generate no growth of capital, they do provide steady income and will offset high fluctuation in your investment portfolio.

- Money Market Funds can be used instead of Certificates of Deposit. They are more convenient than CDs and have minimum deposits as low as $500. They also offer high current yields and can be liquidated immediately, without any penalties. While the money invested in a Money Market account is not guaranteed by the federal government, it can be considered a safe investment as Money Markets diversify their holdings among prime commercial paper, Treasury Bills, and bank Certificates of Deposit.

- Treasury Bills or T-Bills are short-term securities that mature in one year or less. Treasury bills historically match inflation and are considered a safe place to put your money because they are backed by the U.S. government. The interest paid on these bills is the difference between the purchase price and the amount you receive at maturity.

- Treasury Notes and Treasury Bonds are similar to T-Bills, except they have maturities ranging from one to ten years and may be purchased in denominations as low as $1,000. They pay a fixed rate of interest every six months until the note matures. One difference between notes and bonds is that notes mature in more than one year, but not more than 10 years, from their issue date. Bonds, on the other hand, mature in more than 10 years.

When purchasing bonds, follow these seven strategies:
- Seek expertise.
- Watch price volatility.
- Ladder your maturities.
- Compare interest rates.
- Don't chase yields.
- Look for short maturity.
- Consider tax effects.

Mutual Funds

Now that you have seen the difference between stocks and bonds, let's discuss mutual funds. For the small investor, mutual funds may be the investment of choice. They are opportunities for individual investors to share ownership of groups of stocks and bonds. If you want to invest in stocks, you can choose a stock fund; if you like bonds, you can choose a bond fund.

You can also invest in an asset allocation fund or a "balanced" fund (explained later on in this chapter) that diversifies the investment for you in just one fund. These can be good starter funds or one-stop shopping funds for investors who want broad choices.

Mutual funds are also classified by their objectives; for example, an "income fund" will invest in assets that pay regular income or a "growth fund" will concentrate on providing growth of principal. These types of funds can consist of all small companies or all large companies. An additional big plus is that your investment is spread over many companies or agencies. Here are the benefits and conveniences of investing in mutual funds.

Benefits of Mutual Funds:
- Portfolio Diversification: All your "eggs are not in one basket."
- Full-Time Professional Management: Someone who knows what s/he is doing is taking care of your money.
- Liquidity: You have quick access to cash if needed.

Conveniences of Mutual Funds:
- Flexible Investment Methods

- Lump Sum Deposit: Allows you to invest a reenlistment bonus.
- Periodic Deposits: Allow you to invest sea pay, hazardous duty pay, deployment pay, etc.
- Dollar-Cost Averaging: Allows fewer shares to be purchased when the value is high and more shares to be purchased when the value is low. Also avoids the need to "time" the market. This strategy is a lot safer and easier than trying to determine when a stock has hit its low or high point.
- Automatic Bank Draft Investing: Same amount of money is invested every month, thereby creating a habit for you.
- Low Investment Minimums (this is good for military personnel).
- From as little as $100 to $1,000 is needed to open an account.
- Add as little as $25 to $50 monthly—automatically from your checking account.
- Exchange Privileges: Able to transfer your investments within the same fund group.
- Check-Writing Privileges: Many give you the ability to write checks against your mutual fund account.

Mutual Funds Designed For Income

- U.S. Government Securities Funds: These are funds whose portfolios are invested solely in securities that are obligations of the U.S. government, its agencies, and/or its instrumentalities. The primary objective of these funds is current income. Although government funds are some of the most conservative funds offered, as with other bond funds, the net asset value will fluctuate with interest rate changes.
- Municipal Bond Funds: Municipal bond funds are those funds whose portfolios consist of bonds issued by state and local governments and other tax-exempt entities, and whose interest income is exempt from federal income taxes (and in some instances from city and state taxes). The prime objective in this fund type is tax-free income, although limited growth is possible

by reinvesting distributions. The net asset value of this type of fund will also fluctuate with changes in interest rates.

- Corporate Bond Funds: These mutual funds' portfolios invest primarily in senior securities, such as corporate bonds, notes, or preferred stocks. Generally, this fund type has a primary objective of current income, with capital growth as a secondary consideration. However, there are some fixed income funds, such as convertible bond funds, that generate limited current income and are geared more toward capital growth. The net asset value in this type of fund will fluctuate with changes in interest rates.

- High Yield Corporate Bond Funds: These bond funds invest primarily in lower quality corporate bonds in order to generate high current income. These "junk" bonds are issued by companies that are currently out of favor with the financial markets. As a result, they generally have a higher interest rate or are issued at a deep discount from their maturity value. In addition to the higher interest rate, to offset the higher risks associated with this fund type, most high yield bond funds offer broad diversification among many issues and companies. As with other bond funds, the net asset value of this type of fund will fluctuate with interest rate changes.

Mutual Funds Designed For Growth

There are a few traditional funds you can invest in so your money grows faster:

- Balanced/Flexible Funds: This fund type has the primary objectives of both income and capital appreciation consistent with reasonable risk. The portfolio will hold varying ratios of stocks and bonds. During periods of market volatility, these funds tend to be the most stable of all equity funds.

- Growth and Income Funds: This type of fund invests mainly in the common stock of companies that have had a track record of increasing market value and that also have a solid record of paying dividends. These funds attempt to combine long-term capital growth with a steady stream of dividend income.

- Growth Funds: Growth funds typically invest in stocks of established companies in growing industries and/or companies moving upward within their own industries. The primary objective of such funds is capital growth; dividend income is a secondary or incidental consideration. These funds generally invest in stocks on a long-term basis and may therefore have less volatile price fluctuations than aggressive growth funds. As with aggressive growth funds, an investment in this fund type should be made for the long term.
- Aggressive Growth Funds: Also known as Maximum Capital Gains Funds, their solid objective is to seek aggressive growth. Generally, fund portfolios may be comprised of stock from speculative or relatively small, little known, emerging growth companies. Because of this investment philosophy, the value of this type of fund may fluctuate more rapidly than the stock market as a whole. Investment in this type of fund should be made for the long term by more aggressive investors.

Specialized Funds

These types of mutual funds concentrate their investments in specific industries or a group of industries, in special types of securities, or in regional investments. Because there is more emphasis in one target area, these funds can be more volatile than more fully diversified mutual fund portfolios. If they are invested in a growth industry, however, they can also yield a high return on your investment.

- International Funds: These funds are designed to take advantage of growth situations abroad. Three different types of international funds fall into this category:
- Foreign Funds have at least 65% of their portfolio invested in foreign securities.
- Global Funds buy both foreign and U.S. securities.
- Regional Funds specialize in securities from a specific geographic area or a country outside the United States.

Individual Investment Accounts

A number of the accounts we will discuss have favorable tax advantages, which are available if the funds are held until retirement:

- Individual Retirement Account (IRA) is a popular means for putting away money that is tax-deductible and tax-deferred. For tax purposes, depending on how much you earn, you may be eligible to deduct your IRA contribution from your taxable income. Penalties exist for withdrawal of money from your traditional IRA before you reach the age of 59½ years. Therein lay the potential problem: with a traditional IRA, you are penalized if you withdraw any money prior to age 59½.

- Roth IRA: This plan has its own rules. When contributing to a Roth IRA, you do not get a tax break when you deposit money into the account, but if you withdraw the money after age 59½, it is tax-free. That is a great advantage for individuals who are young because it allows them a lot of time to build their financial security. The Roth IRA has some special features. For instance, you can take your original contributions out of a Roth IRA any time you like and pay no tax or penalty. If you have the Roth IRA for more than five years, you may also withdraw the money if you become fully disabled or if you are using the money to buy your first home ($10,000 lifetime limit) or to pay for college. You will have to pay taxes on that withdrawal if it is more than your original contribution, but you will not be subject to the penalty for premature withdrawal.

- 403(b) plan is a special type of employee retirement savings plan, also known as a tax-sheltered annuity that is available only to employees of educational institutions and other qualifying non-profit organizations.

- An Annuity is a financial contract that is sold by an insurance company. It provides an investment opportunity that will grow tax-deferred (you won't have to pay taxes on it) and which has insurance components that will cover the replacement of the dollars invested. Annuities can be used to supplement your retirement plan.

You or your spouse may have the choice of an annuity through your work, or you can purchase an annuity individually. Annuities provide certain services, depending on the specific language in the contract. The contract involves many players as outlined below:

o   The contract owner is the person who makes the contract with the insurance company and who invests the money.

o   The annuitant is the person who received the income benefits from the annuity when activated. The income period ranges from lifetime to a specific time frame.

o   The beneficiary is the individual named by the owner of the contract who will receive the benefits of the annuity should the contract owner die. A contingent beneficiary should also be named in the event that the beneficiary dies during the build-up.

• Thrift Savings Plan is a plan that usually requires an after-tax contribution that is either fully or partially matched by the employer's contribution. There is no immediate tax benefit to this plan. You do, however, get the monies contributed by your employer and the plan accumulates tax-deferred.

• Individuals or couples can open brokerage accounts, or they can be opened by the "brokers" who represent the investor and who will buy and sell the investment according to the investor's wishes. These accounts provide an opportunity for buying and selling investment identities. The brokerage firm can hold the investment, or the share certificates can be issued to the individual. There are several ways a brokerage account can be managed, so asking good questions about how the broker makes money, whether there are expenses associated with having the brokerage account, and whether there are restrictions with owning an account is a good idea.

Picking an Investment Manager/Financial Planner

If you decide to use an Investment Manager/Financial Planner, spend time researching his/her performance. Also, for a variety of reasons, be very careful about using members of your family or your spouse's family.

Chapter Eight

Insurance and Protection

Of all the topics covered in this book, insurance will be the least popular. Why? Because no one wants to think about paying money for a loss you don't want to experience. Obviously, death is certain; we just do not know when that might happen.

For many individuals, insurance is a "necessary evil" that they hope is never needed. Insurance is meant to reduce or manage the financial risks that may and will come along someday. The reason to have insurance is to protect you and your loved ones against unwanted losses. There are many types of insurance: health, disability, life, long-term care, automobile, house or renters', and business (for those of you who have a business on the side). In this chapter, we will cover all but business insurance.

Health Insurance

There are many types of medical or health insurance coverage and while you are in the service, this coverage is provided by the military to protect you and your family. If you are married and your spouse also has health insurance coverage, you can be covered by both policies, with yours being primary and your spouse's being secondary.

Life Insurance

Some questions you should ask are:
- What will my survivors live on if I die?
- How will my funeral expenses get paid if I do not have life insurance?
- Will I continue to need the same amount of insurance as I age?
- How much insurance do I need and how do I assess my needs?

- How do I budget for the amount of insurance for which I need to apply?
- What type of insurance is best for my needs and risk tolerance?

Life insurance is intended to cover income lost, the stay-at-home spouse's "services lost," and the loss of both parents. It is also designed to pay for funeral expenses.

Income Lost Life Insurance

In most cases, you'll want to replace all of the income that's lost when an employed spouse dies. To be more precise, you'll only want to include the after-tax pay and make adjustments for expenses (like a second car) that are incurred from earning that income. Don't forget to add the value of health insurance or other employee benefits to the income number (e.g., how much will it cost to buy it?).

Equation for Calculating Annual Lost Income:

Annual After-Tax Salary   _____
Annual Expenses Directly Related to Deceased
(e.g., clothes, food, memberships, car, and insurances)   − _____
Annual Expenses Paid Off by Other Insurances
(e.g., loans and credit cards)   − _____

Total Annual Lost Income   = _____

Now that you have an amount of income that will need to be replaced each year (since life insurance is often paid off in a lump sum), you need to plan for the beneficiary to invest the life insurance proceeds and spend the income that it generates.

So how do you calculate how big a lump sum you'll need to create a specific annual income? The calculation requires simple division. Take the amount of annual income you want and divide it by the investment return you'd expect to earn on the lump sum (i.e., life insurance proceeds). For instance, if you needed $50,000 a year and thought that you could earn

5% on the money, you'd need a lump sum of $1,000,000 ($50,000 divided by .05 = $1,000,000). That $1,000,000 would provide $50,000 to spend each year without touching your principal.

The investment return that you use will make a big difference in the calculation. For instance, if you assumed a 7% return, you'd only need a lump sum of $714,000.

Note: When you consider how much money you'll need, be sure to take inflation into account. Even a modest 3% annual inflation rate will cut the amount your income will buy in half every 24 years. So, if you lose a spouse in your 30s, your dollar will lose half its value before you retire.

What investment rate should you pick? It should probably be something between CDs on the low end and the long-term stock returns (6 to 8 percent) on the high end. Being conservative is vital.

It is best to overestimate your needs a little. Yes, you'll be buying and paying for a little more insurance than you need, but if you underestimate, you won't realize your mistake until it's too late.

Stay-At-Home Spouse "Services Lost" Life Insurance

If a stay-at-home spouse dies, the target lump sum is a little harder to determine. Unless there's someone like a grandparent who could move in and take over, the survivor will need to pay to have household things done, and that can get expensive. Add up laundry, cleaning, cooking, daycare, and a hundred other daily chores and you have an idea of what the at-home spouse's "salary" is that needs to be replaced. Once you've figured this out, you can then calculate the necessary lump sum like you did for the employed spouse above.

Equation for Calculating Annual Increased Expenses:

Increased Costs   _____
(e.g., childcare costs, housekeeping, and bill paying)
Annual Expenses Directly Related to Deceased   – _____
(e.g., clothes, food, memberships, car, and insurances)

Annual Expenses Paid Off by Other Insurances   – _____
(e.g., loans and credit cards)

Total Annual Increased Expenses   = _____

Now use the same calculations as found under the "Income Lost" section above to calculate the "lump sum" of insurance needed.

Loss of Both Parents Life Insurance

You should also consider what would happen if both parents should die while the children are small. Hopefully, you have someone who has agreed in advance to raise your children. If so, the question becomes: how much is needed to allow the children's guardians to house the children (bedroom addition, bigger home) plus take on the extra expense of feeding, clothing, and schooling the children?

Funeral Expenses Life Insurance

Most all of these expenses are covered for service men and women by the military unless you want special services. However, if you opt for something different from the basic military funeral using a military burial site and a standard casket and service, you will have to cover all additional costs.

For example, if you are not using a military plot, you will have to cover the cost of a plot. In addition, you will have to cover part of the cost to move the body. All costs associated with funerals for members of your family, however, will have to be covered by you.

One final thought: you will also want to make sure that the insurance policy is set up properly. Choosing the correct owner and beneficiary can have important consequences. Sitting down with an insurance professional and seeking advice on how your insurance policy should be set up is very important.

Term vs. Whole Life

The most common types of insurance you will hear about are "term" and "whole life." Many hybrids or various combinations of the two also exist. When you buy whole life insurance, you may hear it referred to as permanent, straight life, or ordinary life insurance. This type of policy will cover a person for his/her entire lifetime and will produce a cash value.

The premium and death benefit is the same throughout the time the insured owns the policy. Universal life insurance is also a form of whole life insurance. The difference between whole life and universal insurance is that the premium and cash value of the latter will fluctuate over time and needs to be monitored on an annual basis. Term insurance is purchased for a specific period of time. It will not build cash value and it pays a specified dollar amount if the policyholder dies. Term insurance may or may not be renewable or converted to whole life insurance.

So what's the difference between term and whole life insurance?

Term Life

These policies offer a death benefit only and usually cost a lot less because you are only paying for the insurance for a specific time frame, most commonly 10, 20, or 30 years. Such policies are pure insurance; all that you are buying is insurance. There are no special effects, bells, or whistles associated with a term life policy. As a result, this type of insurance is less expensive than whole life insurance, but the premiums will increase as the policyholder gets older. That's because the premiums are based on the age of the insured.

With term insurance, you can choose:

- An annual renewal term premium option, which means the policy provides protection for one year and must be renewed each year. The premium increases annually, based on your age. Alternatively, you can choose a level premium for a set number of years.
- Level term, which provides protection for a specified number of years, usually 5 to 20 years. Premiums remain stable throughout that period.
- Decreasing term, which provides protection each year for a fixed premium, but the amount of coverage decreases annually. Mortgage insurance is an example of this type of coverage.
- Convertible term, which allows you to convert to a cash value policy.

Term insurance should be purchased with a guaranteed renewable feature. This means that the insurance company must renew the contract at normal rates—not rates based on health problems—until a stated age. You should also be sure to ask for a convertible policy in case you want to change the type of insurance from term to whole life or permanent.

Whole Life

These insurance policies offer death benefits with policy reserves, better known as cash values. This type of life insurance is more expensive than term protection because you are paying not only for insurance, but also for the potential savings plan or cash value and the internal administrative costs the insurance company will charge you.

The cash value grows tax-deferred and can be accessed in emergencies or at retirement. Be aware that these cash values should be cashed in only in the event of an emergency and could become a taxable event. This will result in a lower death benefit if you die before you pay back the borrowed money. You will be charged interest on the loan and the policy could expire with no value if not paid back. Several types of permanent life insurance exist:

Traditional Whole Life: The premium on this type of insurance is a fixed amount because the cost of the policy is spread over a longer period of time. Some of the premium dollars are invested to build cash value. Therefore, the selection of insurance companies is very important. Traditional whole life policies are the most conservative type of policy and you should use a carrier with excellent financial ratings that specializes in this type of policy.

Universal Life Insurance is thought to be more flexible than your traditional whole life insurance. The premiums on this type of insurance are flexible and the amount of coverage is adjustable. The coverage amount can also be increased or decreased without the insured individual having to show proof of insurability again.

When the first premium is paid, the insured can make additional payments to increase the investment potential and the accumulated cash value. As with traditional whole life insurance, the accumulated savings are tax-deferred. These monies can be borrowed against and the interest earned is determined by the Money Market rates. These aspects can make this type of insurance more competitive than whole life.

Variable Life

Variable Life Insurance is very different from whole life insurance because it allows the policyholder to decide where the cash in the policy is invested, thereby shifting the burden from the insurance company to the insured. The investment choices for variable life policies consist of stocks, bonds, and mutual funds. There's a guaranteed minimum death benefit and any amounts earned above the face value are credited to the policyholder.

Also, while better potential for accumulation of your cash value exists, there is the risk that a person who is unfamiliar with investing may do worse with a variable policy than with a whole life policy. Therefore, the cash value of the policy may also decrease. As with the other types of life insurance, the savings accumulate tax-deferred and borrowing against them is permitted. The amount you borrow will be deducted from the benefit paid to your beneficiary if you die prior to paying the money back.

One common unethical practice in the insurance industry is "churning." This is when your insurance agency will encourage you to replace your existing cash value insurance policy with a new one, not because you need the coverage but because they will earn a big commission from selling you that new policy. The commission agents earn from their sales can range from 10 to 100 percent, depending on the type of insurance you buy. Sitting down with an honest agent is the best way to "insure" you will make the right decision for your family and yourself.

Never cancel an existing life insurance policy unless, or until, you obtain a new policy elsewhere. Another important issue to consider is your beneficiary designation. Typically, when you apply for and obtain insurance, you name a person who will be your beneficiary upon your death, usually your spouse or your parents. As time passes and things change (you get married, divorced, or have children) you will want to change the beneficiary. Many times this important task is forgotten and the wrong person is your beneficiary when you die.

Long-Term Care Insurance

This type of insurance provides coverage for individuals with chronic disabilities. This coverage has become more popular because Medicare and Supplemental Insurance do not address this issue. It covers issues you may think you don't need to be concerned with unless you are "old." The need for long-term care insurance is now coming to light, however, because the families of the elderly are facing the concerns of entire life savings being put at risk. That's because these savings must be used up before Medicaid kicks in. An additional concern of this type of insurance is the question of if you buy it will you even use it? And if you do use it, how long of a coverage period did you purchase?

Long-term care insurance provides services to you if you suffer from chronic illness, a disability, or problems with motor skills. The key word is services, not cure or heal. The long-term care provider may need help with your routine (i.e., dressing, bathing, taking medication, continence, eating, and getting around). These services could be provided at home or at an adult daycare facility, nursing home, or skilled care facility.

Automobile Insurance

This insurance is the most recognized since most states require you to carry at least liability insurance. They also typically require proof of insurance, which satisfies the requirement for financial responsibility if you are involved in an accident.

Types of auto insurance coverage you may want to purchase include:

- Liability insurance, which covers damage you may cause to another person or his/her property.
- Comprehensive insurance, which covers damage to your automobile from vandalism, theft, natural disasters, and fire.
- Collision insurance, which covers damage to your automobile and property resulting from an accident that you caused or someone else caused, but who does not have insurance that will cover the damage to your car or property.

What to ask yourself:
- Do I have the coverage required by the state to meet the minimum mandated by law?
- Do I have the money to replace or repair my automobile if damaged or totaled?
- Can I be responsible for any losses I might cause to others?
- Do I live a fast-paced lifestyle that consists of unsafe driving, which might cause my insurance cost to go up?
- Do I want to take the risk of becoming involved in a serious accident that I do not have the coverage or money to pay for?

Homeowner or Renters' Insurance

If you own your home, it is probably your largest asset and debt. The risk is that your home and other property are subject to many potential types of losses. Fire, theft, vandalism, accident, or negligence all place the value of that asset at risk. Homeowner insurance covers these types of damages.

Many levels of insurance coverage and benefits exist. The cost of insurance is based on how much of that risk you are willing to assume in the event of a loss. For example, you can maintain a deductible amount that you will pay before your coverage kicks in (e.g., $100, $500, and $1,000). The higher the deductible, the lower the premium.

Renters should be concerned with the cost of replacing property in their rental unit should a fire, theft, vandalism, accident, or negligence occur. Sounds familiar, doesn't it? Just because you do not own the property you live in does not mean you should not protect what you own within that property. Moreover, you need to protect yourself from any liability the owner of the property may place on you in the event of damage to their property.

What to ask yourself:
- If I own property, can I afford to repair or replace it if damaged?
- What potential harm could happen to someone in my home?
- How much coverage do I need and can I afford?

- Do I have valuables that should have special coverage?
- As a renter, what does my landlord cover and what is my responsibility?

Remember, you have many options when purchasing insurance. Know what you need to know in order to protect your assets and review your requirements on an annual basis.

Chapter Nine

Retirement

You may neglect a number of things in your life, but do not neglect retirement planning. If you do, you may end up working way beyond your desired retirement age or living well below the standard of living you desire. Overlooking the importance of planning for your own retirement is possibly the biggest mistake you can make.

Only about one third of you will take the time to calculate your retirement needs. The American Savings Education Council says people who calculate their needs are far more likely to hit the target than those who just plunk an arbitrary amount into a Thrift Savings Plan. Unfortunately, too many people guess and shortchange themselves.

Perhaps people underestimate their future needs because they're doing a poor job of saving for retirement. In that case, maybe they'd rather not know how far off the mark they are. In addition, most military personnel don't worry about retirement because they think they're going to retire from the military. Unfortunately, less than half of those who enter the military stay in until retirement.

So, how do you go about assessing your future income needs? Is it as simple as determining 70 or 90 percent of your current income? No, there's that pesky inflation factor that must also be considered. What return will your savings and investments generate? Will there be a long "bear" stock market in your saving or retirement years? Do you want to travel the world and stay at first-class hotels or would you be happy just renting an RV and visiting Mount Rushmore and other national treasures?

All those considerations are just for starters. If you really want to get a grip on what you'll need for retirement, talk with an advisor, such as a certified financial planner. Remember, your life should control your finances; your finances should not control your life.

Spend time telling your advisor what you'd like your life to be like during retirement. They'll then tell you what you need to fund it. When you meet with an advisor, be ready to spend a significant amount of time talking about what you've learned about money, what you're passionate about, what you want to do, etc.

If you went to the doctor tomorrow and found out you only have five years to live—and you'd be in pretty good health until then—you'd ask yourself, "What would I like to do in the next five years?" Whatever is incorporated into that answer is what your financial planner should take into consideration.

It's important to add a historical perspective when calculating retirement needs. That's because you can't assume that history won't repeat itself when it comes to the economy. Today's (2004) stock markets are extremely overvalued by historical standards—much more so than they were in 1929. The market could collapse or go sideways for 10 years. Look at Japan. We used to think they would take over the world. In the 1980s their market went up threefold; in the 1990s it collapsed threefold.

Retirement is based on assumptions: you assume that you will be able to retire at a certain age; you assume that you will have a certain amount of income; you assume that your investments will garner a certain percent return; and you apply an assumed average inflation rate. If any one of those assumptions is incorrect, it will throw off your entire plan.

The most common way to look at retirement is to think about the three-legged stool. Think of that stool as consisting of one leg that represents your pension, another leg that represents your Social Security or Federal Employees' Retirement Plan, and a third leg that represents your personal savings and investments.

The first two legs are wobbly at best. We already addressed the fact that less than half of all military personnel actually retire from the military. We've also mentioned that few private sector firms provide a pension plan; so, there goes the pension leg of the stool. The federal government has played with the Social Security funds and the baby boomers may drain it dry. That leaves your personal savings as the main source for your secure financial retirement.

When you view it this way, no matter what your income, achieving retirement goals will require years of planning. One of the biggest myths about retirement planning is that you need a lot of money to have a plan for the future. That is simply not true. You need the plan so that when you do have excess cash, you will already have the plan set in place to get started.

To retire comfortably is tougher in today's environment than it was in the past. There are three areas that should be kept in mind while you are planning for your secure future:

1. Long Life: Today, when a person lives to be 65, s/he can be considered middle-aged. Realistically, s/he should plan to live another 25 to 30 years and many individuals may live to be 100. Therefore, when planning to retire at age 65, realize that you will only work for 35 to 45 years. During that time, you will have to accumulate enough savings to last 25 years or more.

    Some of you young service men and women may be thinking that's too far off for me to think about now. The fact is that American men and women typically live 75 years or more. And, because of current medical studies, that number is expected to rise. It may well exceed 100 years for your generation.

2. Inflation: Inflation is the erosion of the purchasing power of your dollar over time. Inflation arises from the fact that from one year to the next, it takes more money to buy the same thing. A car today costs significantly more than it did 10 years ago.

    Inflation is firmly entrenched in our economy and makes it more difficult to accumulate resources in advance of retirement. It also makes it harder to maintain an adequate living standard over the course of a long retirement. Here is a calculation to think about: if there is an inflation factor of 3.5 percent per year, the dollar you spend today will need to be two dollars in twenty years to achieve the same purchasing power. That means if your standard of living today is based on $35,000 a year, in twenty years, you will need an income of $70,000 in order to spend the same amount of money on the same items. So, you see, with even a modest rate of inflation, you may witness your cost of living double or even triple during your retirement years.

3. Increased Dependence on Personal Savings: As mentioned before, working people will have to rely more on their personal savings for retirement funds. With fiscal pressures on the government and employers, investors will find that their pensions, Social Security, and Federal Employees' Retirement Plans may not live up to their expectations. That leaves the final factor, unrealistic expectations.

A few of you may have had your expectation bubble burst these last several years in the stock market. Prior to the decline of the financial market, many individuals expected to retire without a decline in their income. Unfortunately, however, they found that they now might have to scale back their spending when they retire and live on less than they thought they would. Alternatively, they will have to retire later in life. Your expectations will dictate the amount of savings and investments you will need when you retire.

Four Steps to Successful Retirement Planning

Realizing what it may take to successfully accumulate the necessary funds for retirement is a first step. The sooner you take the plunge and begin planning for retirement, the better the chances you will have of being able to get where you want to go. The time to start planning is right now. There are four primary steps that must be implemented if you want to be successful with your planning. They are:

1. Determining what income you will need during retirement;
2. Determining how much you will need to accumulate in order to have a secure retirement;
3. Reviewing your progress periodically since things may change each year; and
4. Checking the resources you have now and determining what to add for success.

Determine What Income You Will Need During Retirement

If you have many years before you retire, determining your income needs may not be on your mind right now. However, you need to pay more attention and prepare today for your quality of life at retirement. As we discussed, it is likely that you will spend more than one third of your life in retirement, living on the money you saved and invested while working.

Once you have determined how and where you want to live when you retire, you can then estimate your expenses, first in today's dollars and then in future or inflated dollars. There is a rule of thumb you should use when determining that amount: to maintain the same standard of living in retirement that you enjoy today, you will need approximately 75 to 85 percent of the amount you currently spend.

If you are under the age of 30, you will enjoy the luxury of many years in which to save and invest. If you are closer to retirement age (10 to 15 years away), however, you should prepare a detailed spreadsheet of your living expenses and budget as soon as possible. Doing this will bring home your true needs. Remember, there will be some expenses that will decrease or go away when you retire. As a result, working through your cash flow will be an exercise that reveals where additional financial needs, such as healthcare and travel, will be necessary.

One of the biggest mistakes you may make in planning for retirement is either ignoring or underestimating the effects of inflation. I know I have already mentioned inflation, but I can't stress enough its importance. Even though it is much lower now than it was during the double-digit years spanning 1979 to 1981, inflation still erodes your purchasing power. When you retire, much of your income may be fixed, causing it to lag behind inflation. Thus, you should consider inflation as important from now until the day you retire and even on though your retirement years.

Determine How Much You Will Need to Have a Secure Retirement

Once you estimate how much yearly income you will need when you retire, you will then need to figure out how much of that amount you will need to accumulate personally in addition to your other sources of income, such as pension benefits and Social Security.

Use a spreadsheet to calculate your needs by taking into account your projected life expectancy and the inflation factor we discussed. Unfortunately, projection of inflation while planning is only the beginning. By the time you reach retirement age, you will once again calculate an inflation factor so that your purchasing power does not decrease while you're in retirement.

Review Your Progress Periodically Since Things May Change Each Year

To start this process, total the assets you own now that will be used when you retire. Remember, all of the assets that are not targeted toward college or a vacation home should be earmarked toward your retirement assets to be used to support you and your spouse in your golden years. Don't include the value of your home unless you plan on selling it. Furthermore, don't include your personal property, furniture, or automobiles. Chances are you will not be able to sell such items for their true value; that is if you would even want to.

A good strategy is to plan on having your mortgage paid off by the time you retire. Doing so will lower your living expenses. In retirement, you will not want to be tied to a big home loan or a high rent.

Check the Resources You Have and Determine What to Add for Success

This process requires you to do your homework. Once you follow these steps, you will come to the realization that you do not have enough money to meet your retirement income needs. You will then see the changes that are necessary in helping you increase your investment assets. Remember, the best way to increase your assets is to increase your participation in your Thrift Savings Plan. The fact that the plan is tax-deferred makes it the best place for long-term investments.

Early Retirement

As a service member, if you join the military right out of high school and serve until you retire, you will be an average age of less than 50 years old. That will be considered early retirement.

That may sound great but it will compound your problem. Not only will you be looking at what you are going to do with the rest of your life but, if you truly want to "retire," you face the problem of having to accumulate sufficient resources to fund a longer period of retirement. As a result, personal savings and investments play an even more important role for the early retiree.

These same problems arise if early retirement is forced upon you. It is possible to retire early with the proper planning, taking advantage of the opportunities available to you and doing the projections and the hard work required to be successful. Who can afford to retire early? There are two types of people who have the characteristics of a successful planner:

Early and consistent planners—These people realize that it will take years and years of planning to succeed. They begin at age 20 or 30 and never stop. They take advantage of the retirement plans offered to them through the military and/or their employers. They avoid stopping and starting their investments. They assess and adjust their investments based on what is happening in their lives.

Those who are willing to sacrifice today—These types of people spend less to achieve a secure financial future while in retirement. The fact that most people can't even save $25.00 a month during their working years is a characteristic that makes it difficult to successfully plan for retirement.

If you want to be a successful early retiree, you must save a minimum of 10 to 20 percent of your income during your working years. You need to be an expert at living below your means. Live in inexpensive housing and keep your living expenses low. Don't buy all that "stuff" that you think you can't live without; it only takes money away from your investments. Furthermore, keep those strategies once you're retired.

If you are successful and are able to retire early, there are some costs that you might not be aware of and which may prompt you to reconsider early retirement. They are:

- Health Insurance: If you are taking early retirement, the big question is: are you covered for medical expenses until age 65? Health insurance is very expensive and if you have to purchase an individual policy, you need to factor in that expense in your retirement planning.

- Part-time Employment: If you are counting on working part-time when you retire as a way of supplementing your retirement income, this tactic could prove risky. You may not earn enough money to cover your expenses, your health may make working difficult, and there may not be jobs available.
- Reduced Social Security or Federal Employee Benefits: If you are planning to receive benefits, they may not be available in the amounts you expect. This could be a result of retiring early and the calculation of a lower initial benefit amount. It might also result from how the government manages these funds.
- Consequences Involving Your Other Benefits: If you have other funds set aside to add to your retirement benefits, they may be affected by your decision to retire early, too. Not only will you have fewer years to contribute to your funds, but there may also be penalties incurred if you withdraw funds prior to age 59½ years. You should consult a tax advisor before you make any retirement decisions.

Thrift Savings Plan

As a service man or woman, you have the Thrift Savings Plan available to you to invest in for retirement. The Thrift Savings Plan (TSP) is a federal government-sponsored retirement savings and investment plan. Congress established the TSP in the Federal Employees' Retirement System Act of 1986. The purpose of the TSP is to provide retirement income.

On October 30, 2000, the Floyd D. Spence National Defense Authorization Act for fiscal year 2001 (Public Law 106-398) was signed into law. One provision of the law extended participation in the TSP, which was originally designed only for federal civilian employees, to members of the uniformed services.

The TSP is a defined contribution plan. The retirement income you receive from your TSP account will depend on how much you have contributed to your account during your working years and on those contributions' earnings. This type of plan is usually very advantageous if you have a long working life and if you, as the participant, contribute enough to build up a substantial retirement fund.

The TSP offers the same type of savings and tax benefits that many private corporations offer their employees under "401(k)" plans. TSP regulations are published in Title 5 of the Code of Federal Regulations, Parts 1600–1690, and are periodically supplemented and amended in the Federal Register.

Why Participate?

If you're young or undecided about your career with the military, it might be easy to ignore suggestions that you start planning for retirement now. If you put in 20 years, you'll have government-issued retirement income to stash in that government-issued footlocker. And, if you separate from service as soon as is humanly possible, you can think about investing in your future at that time. The question is, will you? Time is one of the biggest contributors to a successful retirement investment.

Who Can Participate?

Uniformed members of the Army, Navy, Air Force, Marine Corps, Coast Guard, Public Health Service, and the National Oceanic and Atmospheric Administration who are serving on active duty and members of the Ready Reserve or the National Guard of those services in any pay status can contribute to the TSP. Unlike in the private sector—where employees generally need to work a certain length of time before they can participate in their employer's 401(k) plan—you may begin contributing to the TSP immediately.

When Can I Join?

New members of the uniformed services will have 60 days after joining the service to enroll in the TSP; thereafter, they may enroll during the semi-annual open seasons (April 15–June 30 and October 15–December 31).

Where Are My Contributions Invested?

You can invest any portion of your TSP account in any combination of five TSP investment funds, including:

- Government Securities Investment (G) Fund
- Fixed Income Index Investment (F) Fund
- Common Stock Index Investment (C) Fund
- Small Capitalization Stock Index Investment (S) Fund
- International Stock Index Investment (I) Fund

How Do I Choose the Right Funds?

Those funds may need some decoding before you can understand them. How you invest your money is a financial decision, but several personal factors are involved, too. There are no guarantees that the investments will perform well and provide high returns. Therefore, you need to look at your tolerance for risk. For example, are you willing to take a risk that the small, growing companies included in the Small Capitalization Stock Index Investment Fund will make a profit over time and return it to investors? Or, do you prefer a more conservative approach, such as the Fixed Income Index Investment Fund, which effectively reduces its risk but also lowers its potential for gain by sticking to stocks that offer fixed income?

How Much Can I Contribute?

Each year you can contribute a percentage of the basic pay you earn each month. You may also be able to contribute all or any whole percentage of any special or incentive pay (including reenlistment or other bonuses) you receive. However, the total amount you contribute each year cannot exceed the Internal Revenue Code limit for each calendar year. If you are 50 years of age or older and are already contributing the maximum to your TSP account, you may also make "catch-up" contributions.

If you are a member of the Ready Reserve or the National Guard and you have a civilian TSP account (or another qualified employer plan, such as a 401(k) or 403(b)), the total of all your contributions to all of your plans cannot exceed $13,000 in 2004. If you also participate in a Section 457 plan, consult with your private sector plan administrator concerning any limitation on the amount you can contribute to your TSP account. If we haven't confused you too much, keep reading because your future depends on it!

Are My Contributions Matched?

Probably not, but the law allows that critical military specialties may be designated for matching contributions. Members serving in these specialties who agree to serve for six years will be eligible for matching contributions. Your service can tell you whether or not your specialty has been designated as critical and whether or not you are eligible to contract to receive matching contributions.

Why Should I Have Both the Military Pension and the TSP?

Career military types may wonder why in the world they should save their own money when they'll qualify for military retired pay soon enough. We're here to tell you that things change, and even the most loyal soldier may not make it to 20 years. Your TSP doesn't depend on how many promotions you earn. Plus, it's yours to keep even if you don't serve the 20 years ordinarily necessary to receive military retired pay.

Military retired pay is a defined benefit plan. This means the benefit you receive from the military retirement system is based on your years of service and the rank you hold at the time of your retirement, rather than on the amount of your contributions and earnings. The TSP, on the other hand, is a defined contribution plan, which means the balance in your TSP account will depend on how much you have contributed during your working years and on those contributions' earnings.

What About Loans and Withdrawals?

The TSP is a long-term retirement savings plan that provides special tax advantages. Limitations on withdrawals help ensure that retirement savings will be used for their intended purpose. Because the TSP is a retirement plan, you may be better served if you can avoid borrowing or taking in-service withdrawals from your TSP account. In other words, you will be better off if you continue to allow your contributions to accumulate earnings. Therefore, uniformed services' TSP participants (whether in active service or members of the Ready Reserve or the National Guard) can withdraw funds from their accounts in only two cases:

- Age-based in-service withdrawals for participants who are 59½ or older.
- Financial hardship in-service withdrawals for participants who can document financial hardship.

When you take an in-service withdrawal, you cannot return or repay the money you remove from your account. As a result, you permanently reduce your retirement savings and future earnings on the amount withdrawn. In addition, any contributions you are making to the TSP will be automatically terminated for six months after each financial hardship withdrawal. Thus, before taking an in-service withdrawal, you should evaluate your options to see if a TSP loan would be more beneficial.

The TSP loan program allows you to borrow your own contributions and the attributable earnings from your account as either a general-purpose loan or as a loan to purchase your primary residence. The minimum loan amount is $1,000. The maximum loan amount is $50,000; however, the amount you can borrow may be less, depending on any outstanding TSP loans you have already taken and on certain limits set by the Internal Revenue Code. (If you have both a uniformed services and a civilian TSP account, your account balances will be combined for the purposes of determining the maximum amount you may borrow from either account.) You also pay interest on the amount borrowed. The loan repayment, including interest, will go into your TSP account.

Is There Such a Thing as Withdrawals Without Penalty?

While you are a member of the uniformed services, any tax-deferred money you withdraw before the age of 59½ as a financial hardship in-service withdrawal is subject to the IRS's 10-percent early withdrawal penalty, in addition to regular income tax.

With respect to post-separation withdrawals, if you separate from the military before the year you reach age 55, you can transfer your TSP account to an IRA or other eligible retirement plan (e.g., your 401(k) plan or your civilian TSP account) or you can begin receiving annuity payments without penalty. If you separate from service during or after the year in which you turn age 55, your withdrawals are not subject to the early withdrawal penalty, but you will need to pay income taxes on the money withdrawn.

Should I Maintain an IRA, Too?

Participation in the TSP does not affect your ability to contribute to an Individual Retirement Account (IRA). However, because you are a uniformed services member who is covered by the uniformed services retirement plan, your ability to make income-tax-deductible contributions to an IRA depends upon your income and that of your spouse. Your IRA provider or your tax advisor can give you specific information about the different types of IRAs, the rules affecting each type, and how they apply to your situation.

When I Separate From Service, What Are My Withdrawal Options?

When you separate from the uniformed services, you may:
- Receive a single payment. All or a portion of your account can be transferred to an Individual Retirement Account (IRA) or other eligible retirement plan, such as a 401(k) plan or your civilian TSP account. Tax-exempt contributions to the TSP are not eligible for transfer to an IRA or other eligible retirement plan. These contributions will be paid directly to you. Earnings attributable to the income-tax-exempt contributions, however, are eligible for transfer to an IRA or other eligible retirement plan.
- Request a series of monthly payments based on a dollar amount, a number of months, or your life expectancy. All or a portion of certain monthly payments can be transferred to an IRA or other eligible retirement plan.
- Request a TSP annuity. You must have at least $3,500 in your account in order to purchase an annuity.
- Leave your money in the TSP. You may leave your money in the TSP, where it will continue to accrue earnings. Although you will not be able to continue to make contributions, you will be able to make inter-fund transfers. You must begin withdrawing from your

account no later than April 1 of the year following the year you turn age 70½ and are separated from service.

Because the TSP record-keeper must maintain separate accounts for civilian and uniformed services, participants who are both federal civilian employees and uniformed services members (e.g., Reservists) may have two separate accounts. If you have two accounts, you will need to separately review each one.

I Want a Plan for Retirement. Where Can I Turn for Assistance?

Seek the advice of a financial advisor to help you develop a plan and set goals so that you are better prepared to handle the financial aspects of retirement. They can help you see at a glance what you may need to do about additional saving for things like sending your kids to college or providing life insurance protection for loved ones.

Chapter Ten

Tax Planning

Taxes…you hate taxes, right? Becoming tax savvy and finding sensible ways to save on taxes is a great way to cut expenses. Every taxpayer, no matter how old, can benefit from learning ways to cut his or her taxes. Yet, as with so many financial areas, if you are not educated on the subject, many of you will pay more taxes than you have to, even though you hate paying them.

The law states that Americans have a right to pay only the minimum legal tax and there is nothing wrong with arranging your affairs so as to keep your taxes as low as possible. It is one common thread that unites all Americans, both rich and poor. We all minimize our taxes because no one wants to pay more tax than the law requires. Taxes are enforced and are seldom paid voluntarily.

The year 2004, however, may change the tax season's reputation as the most hated time of the year. That's because back-to-back tax cuts and tens of billions of dollars in retroactive reductions are about to go into effect. All told, the Treasury expects its coffers to end the first half of 2004 $100 billion lighter than if last year's tax cuts had not occurred. Lower withholding is one of the reasons to smile and there is never a better year to get an early start on your return. If you normally owe when you file, you will likely owe less this year and you may even get a refund.

Let's face it; there are many tax strategies and every year the rules change. Sometimes these changes benefit you and sometimes they don't. Not all of them are worth the effort, however, and unfortunately, many may end up costing you more.

In other words, simply because there are legal ways to reduce your tax bill doesn't mean that each and every option will benefit your particular situation. Smart tax planning is to know "when to hold 'em and when to fold 'em." Perhaps the most important thing to remember about tax planning is that it is an important part of your total personal financial planning. Keep in mind, however, that it is just one part. Even though any investment or financial decision should include an evaluation of its tax ramifications, none should be made solely or even primarily on that basis alone.

Note: For some of you, there is very little involved in dealing with taxes because you don't own a home, you don't have children, etc. This means that there are no complicated deductions on your tax forms. Many of the strategies we offer below are designed for those individuals who own homes or property, have children, have tax-deferred investments, etc. Whether you fall into that category or not, it will be good for everyone to read on, even those who won't be able to take advantage of the tax strategies today. That's because the following sections will give you another inspiration to get into investments and to sometimes plan your investments around tax strategies. The tactics described will also be used by you when planning for retirement. Always consult your tax professional before making your personal tax decisions.

Tax Strategies

Tax planning consists of much more than simply taking advantage of all possible deductions. Rather, it consists of developing a coherent, long-term strategy to reduce your taxes over the coming years. Tax planning must be a process you take on year-round. The advantage of doing year-round planning is that you eventually learn to avoid past mistakes. You keep on top of the task as you learn and when you learn, you are far better off. That's because you will make financial decisions on the basis of that learning.

Using Retirement Plans to Reduce Taxable Income

Nobody wants to take in less money, but you can take in less taxable money, meaning the cash is yours, not Uncle Sam's (not yet anyway). Putting money into retirement savings is an easy way to do this. If you're participating in the Thrift Savings Plan, consider increasing the amount you contribute. The money goes into your retirement savings account before taxes are figured, meaning you'll have less income for the IRS to tax. Moreover, the cash left over in your pay will actually be greater than you think. The cash in your Thrift Savings Plan earns interest income-tax-deferred so you don't owe until you take it out (usually when you're in a lower tax bracket). If you haven't yet signed up for the military Thrift Savings Plan, do it now!

Adjust Your Withholding

Adjusting your withholding means changing the number of dependents (exemptions) on your W-4 form. Altering this number will affect how much the military takes out in taxes. There are two primary reasons to adjust your withholding status:

At the end of each year, you are having to write a check to the U.S. government, which means not enough taxes are taken out during the year; or

At the end of each year, you get a sizable refund check, which means the U.S. government took out too much of your money and they, instead of you, got to "play" with it all year long.

Now, in the second case, if you have had bad money habits in the past and are more likely to just spend it, then maybe you want the government to keep taking out too much money. If, on the other hand, you are good at handling and saving your money, then you may want to adjust your withholding.

When you make any changes to your income through retirement account participation, you also need to look at the adjustments to your payroll withholding. In fact, you should review your withholding status as the year-end nears anyway just to make sure you're having the appropriate amount of taxes taken from your paycheck.

If you ended up owing taxes this year and your work and family situation is substantially the same, you should consider having the military take out a bit more in taxes this last quarter. Incremental tax payments made in this way means that you don't have to come up with a big check to the IRS in April.

On the other hand, if you got a big refund this year and are expecting the same next year, fill out a new W-4 today so that won't happen again.

The W-4 worksheet will help you estimate your upcoming tax bill and will assist you in determining just how many exemptions you should claim.

While some people like the "forced savings" of overpaying their federal taxes, do yourself a financial favor by pocketing the cash yourself and putting it into a savings account or a Certificate of Deposit instead of giving Uncle Sam an interest-free loan of your money.

Evaluate Your Investments

For taxpayers who are investing in the stock market to earn extra cash, the last few months of the year are the last chance they'll have to assess their situation and sidestep possible tax costs.

Throughout the year, fund managers sell mutual fund holdings and any profits from those sales will be passed along to shareholders as capital gains distributions. That means that even if your fund's overall value declined, you still could have capital gains on these pass-through distributions. So, unless your mutual fund was for a tax-deferred retirement account, you're likely to owe taxes on these gains.

To find out how much of a tax bite to expect, check with your fund manager. Furthermore, don't make any more investments into the account (we recommend consulting a tax pro on this issue) until after the payout is made. If you buy more shares before then, you'll be setting yourself up for more tax liability because all shareholders—even if they've just owned the shares for a day before the payout date—will get a year's worth of taxable dividends and capital gains distributions.

If, in addition to capital gains distributions, you made money on the sale of a stock or fund earlier in the year, now is the time to re-evaluate your investments to see if you can make use of some less profitable holdings. You may want to sell an investment that just isn't recovering from a slump and use the loss to offset the taxable profit you made earlier.

Maximize Your Deductions

Taxpayers who itemize know that deductions can cut tax bills, but only if you follow the IRS rules. You can only use medical expenses that exceed 7.5 percent of your adjusted gross income. Now is the time to look at the doctor bills you've paid so far this year and see if there are any elective medical procedures you want to schedule between now and Dec. 31 that will get your expenses over the threshold.

Similarly, don't wait until the last minute to make non-cash donations to your favorite charity. Too often, taxpayers who are in a year-end rush to clear out their closets and get the tax break overlook—and undervalue—the items they give away.

Start your giveaway list now. You'll be glad you did come December, when you'll have extra room to hide those holiday gifts, and come April, when your tax bill will be lower thanks to your fourth-quarter tax planning goodwill.

Eighteen Ways to Save on Taxes

1. Interview and hire a reputable tax advisor to offer advice and prepare your taxes. Add the cost of last year's tax help, including the cost of tax software, to your deductible miscellaneous expenses.

2. Keep good records. Improving your tax record-keeping system will help you keep from paying more taxes than you should. Keep a notebook or journal handy to keep track of what you spend on miscellaneous tax-deductible expenses. This strategy will make your information gathering easier at the end of the year.

3. Donate to your favorite charity. Keep your receipts when you make your donation. Most people estimate their charitable cash contributions when tax time comes around. The IRS will disallow these if you do not have written proof. Keep a record or, better yet, write a check.

4. Donate unneeded clothing and other personal items to recognized charities. If you have usable clothing, furniture, or other personal property, donate them to a recognized charity. You can take a tax deduction for the donated items' fair market value by obtaining a receipt from that charity.

5. Make sure your tax advisor calculates your return as married filing jointly and separately if you are married. Sometimes taxpayers will end up paying less in taxes if they file separately.

6. Deduct the points if you bought a home or refinanced one this year. Points on a new mortgage are fully deductible in the year you purchase the home, even if the seller paid them for you. When you refinance your mortgage, points are written off over the life of the loan.

7. Write off moving expenses if you relocated for a deployment or a change of duty at least 50 miles further away from your old house than your old job was. You can claim this deduction even if you do not itemize other deductions.

8. Max out your property tax deductions. If you bought a home this year, check the settlement sheet. If you reimbursed the seller for taxes at closing, you can add the amount to your write-off.

9. Send your return in early if you're receiving a refund. Sending your tax return ahead of time, especially if you're going to get money back, allows you to reinvest your money sooner.

10. Don't report a state refund as income if you didn't itemize deductions last year. The money is tax-free.

11. Don't overlook a state tax payment. If you wrote a check with your state return last spring, add the amount to your state tax write-off on your return.

12. Claim the college tuition deduction if your income is too high for the credits. You can write off up to $3,000 as long as your income doesn't exceed $130,000 on a joint return or $65,000 on an individual one. This may change each year, so check with your tax advisor for specifics.

13. Deduct student loan interest. Up to $2,500 can be written off (even if you don't itemize) as long as your income doesn't exceed $130,000 on a joint return, or $65,000 on an individual return. This may change each year, so check with your tax advisor for specifics.

14. Revive carry-over losses from last year's return. There is a cap of the deduction of net losses left you with a carry-over from last year. You can offset gains received on this year's Schedule D if any more

is left or you can use it to shelter other kinds of income, including your salary.

15. Share job-hunting expenses with Uncle Sam if you or your spouse looked for work last year. Itemize costs for telephone calls, resume advice, and travel as miscellaneous expenses if you were looking for a job in the same line of work. Deduct costs in excess of 2 percent of your adjusted gross income.

16. Don't overstate mutual fund profits. If you sold shares of your mutual funds, be sure you use the right tax basis, including dividends reinvested over time, when calculating your capital gains. Reporting too much gain is a costly error no matter how low the capital gains rate is.

17. If you owe money to the IRS, don't send in your payment before it is due. As long as you have paid enough tax during the year to avoid a penalty, there is no reason to file early if you owe money to the IRS. Keep your money working for you until it is due.

18. Send in an amended return if you are advised that you overpaid taxes in the previous year and are entitled to a refund. But don't wait; there is a time limit on sending in an amended return.

Remember, as sure as there are tax laws that will benefit you, there are also some that will not. And every year things will change. There are professionals who can help you as well as computer programs that can assist those of you who want to prepare them yourself.

We work hard all week to earn "a few bucks." We then get a check that's a fraction of what we earned, primarily because of paycheck withholdings like FICA, Medicare, state taxes, federal taxes, and a whole host of benefit plan withdrawals. The average family in America pays 38% of its total income for all taxes every year, which is more than they pay for food, shelter, and clothes combined. The bottom line is to educate yourself and make the best decision for the best possible outcomes. Some final tips:

- Learn the many ways that are available to reduce your taxes.
- Coordinate your income tax planning with other important personal financial planning areas, including investments and retirement planning.

- Keep in mind the tried-but-true tax-advantaged investments like tax-exempt bonds and buying and holding stock and real estate.
- Maintain complete and well-organized income tax records throughout the year. Your tax record-keeping should be coordinated with your personal record-keeping system.
- Effective income tax planning is both a year-round and multi-year process. Spend some time after tax season—with your advisor, if applicable—planning your income tax strategies over the next five years.

Summary

By Master Chief Petty Officer of the Navy Robert J. Walker, Ret.

In the 1940s a third class petty officer needed permission to marry. It's true. Even less than 25 years ago choices were limited and personal situations were controlled to a point where permission to marry was a requirement.

Jump ahead less than three decades and the choices are overwhelming. Everywhere our men and women turn, credit card offers are thrown at them. These offers of free and easy money are stuffed into mailboxes, sent over the Internet and pop up as incentives for discounts when you walk into shopping centers across the country. People get credit cards with higher limits and even higher fees, interest rates and penalties.

But it is never too late to get control and take your life back, and education is a must! We hope that this book helped you do just that. It has the right message and every household can use it as a financial map to navigate the rights and wrongs of managing money as an individual, with a spouse, or for your family. All you need is commitment to take charge, and to do so today.

Those of you exposed to this book will have the information you need for the rest of your lives to help you recognize your financial situation and apply the best strategy to accomplish your financial goals. It doesn't matter how old you are or where you are positioned financially today. What does matter is that you understand that freedom from financial burden is essential to becoming valuable men and women to your branch of service, country and family.

Today I meet young people who have been bankrupt not once, but twice. The system is failing and our young people pay for the rest of their lives, never quite figuring out how it happened.

It's easy to start down the path to financial success. There is a saying: "Pay yourself first." You've probably heard it before, and this book covered it in the first 20 pages. I've practiced it my entire life, and my wife is an expert at it. I don't know how she did it, but she always did and you can, too. Remember to use this book to make good decisions and help your family reach financial success.

Things may have changed in the last 50 years, but the sacrifices made by our men and women in uniform have not. Never be afraid to ask for help because it's not only your duty to serve our country—it's also your duty to make sure your family is financially stable.

Retired Master Chief Petty Officer of the Navy Robert Walker joined the Navy in 1948, became Chief Petty Officer in 1956, and was chosen as MCPON in 1975. He is an advisor to many of the boards dealing with enlisted personnel and their families, and has been called upon to testify before Congress when enlisted personnel issues arise. He currently serves as an advisory board member to the Pioneer Services Foundation.

Appendix A

Your Credit Score: Are You a Prime or Sub-Prime Borrower?

When it comes to borrowing money, you will probably fit into one of two categories: prime or sub-prime. If you are a "prime" borrower you will have a variety of lending options and can get a lower interest rate. If you are a "sub-prime" borrower you will have fewer options and will usually pay a higher interest rate.

How is This Determined?

While many methods may be used to determine loan approval and cost (or pricing), your credit score will usually determine whether you fit into a prime or sub-prime category. Your credit score is used because it measures the one thing lenders look for: risk.

Virtually all lenders (banks, credit unions, mortgage companies, credit cards or loan companies) want to be cautious and frequently use risk-based pricing, and this pricing is based on your credit score. If you do not have enough credit history, or have missed some payments in the past, lenders will not consider you a "prime" risk and you will not receive their prime rate.

The Auto Insurance Example

An easy way to understand this prime and sub-prime model is to look at car insurance, since the risk assessment used in that industry works pretty much the same way as lending:

- At age 16, auto insurance is very expensive—or sub-prime—due to inexperience. This inexperience leads to a higher risk for the insurance company since there is a higher probability of a claim.

- If the driver proves that he or she is safe (no tickets, accidents, etc.) he or she can expect to be rewarded with lower insurance costs as the years go by, and especially after age 25. Since they have proven themselves able to handle the responsibility, they will move from sub-prime to prime.
- On the other hand, if the driver gets a number of tickets or has many accidents, his or her insurance will remain expensive or could even be cancelled. Only when the person has a number of years of safe driving will his or her insurance rates decrease.

How is My Credit Score Determined?

Going into how credit scores are truly determined is incredibly complicated. Basically, credit scores are calculated with data models and mathematical tables that assign points for different pieces of information. This information doesn't come just from banks, loan companies, or credit card companies—utility companies (including cable or satellite), furniture stores, electronic stores, and many others will post information on your credit report. You are responsible for making sure they accurately report your successes (making payments on time) and your shortcomings (late payments or charge-offs).

Each of the three big credit bureaus—Equifax, Experian and TransUnion—use slightly different models and tables, but most of the current scoring systems rely on information in consumer credit bureau reports. The most familiar of these is FICO, which was developed by Fair, Isaac & Co. in the late 1950's. The specific calculations used are unknown (the Federal Trade Commission does not require disclosure of the formulas or methods), but credit-scoring models consider many factors, including but not limited to:

- Delinquencies, late payments, charge-offs, and/or bankruptcy— These will have a negative effect on your score.
- The length of time you've had credit accounts (such as credit cards, loans, etc.)—The longer you've had an account and successfully made payments, the better.

- How many credit accounts you have paid off as agreed—This will have a positive effect on your score.
- Making many requests for credit—If you apply for a car loan at 6 different companies it might be viewed as a higher risk.
- Using almost all of the credit you have available—Higher debt ratios (the amount you owe compared to the amount you make) have a negative effect on your score.
- Length of time at present residence—The longer, the better.
- Your employment longevity and history—The more stable, the better.

Each customer can have three separate scores computed by each of the three bureaus, and each score may be a little different. Some lenders use just one of these three scores, while other lenders look at all three and use the middle score.

What Credit Score Do I Need to Get the Prime Rate?

There is no set score since different lenders require different scores to determine prime and sub-prime borrowers. Credit scores are numeric values that generally range from 300 to 850, and it is generally agreed that less than 620 is considered risky, 620 to 660 is uncertain, and 660 to 770 is considered acceptable.

Just like most sports, the higher the score, the better—if you have a higher score you have a better chance of receiving a lender's prime rate. As scores decrease, the lender's risk increases. A lower score will likely be viewed as a sub-prime risk and the cost of obtaining credit will increase.

According to BankRate.com, FICO scores below 500 can expect the higher prices or interest rates (sub-prime) and those above 720 can expect the lowest prices or interest rates (prime).

How Does My Military Service Affect My Credit Score?

Frequent moves, deployments or TDY result in shorter durations at a single location and can cause multiple credit relationships in many cities. Relocation can also lead to poor credit histories because of an accidentally unpaid utility or medical bill, or an unknown charge-off from a retailer that did not receive a final payment.

Also, some retailers and small loan companies in military communities do not report to a credit bureau, so very positive payment history may not be contained in the FICO score. This means that many military families receive lower scores even though that score may not truly reflect their complete history. These lower scores tend to reflect higher risk and result in sub-prime pricing.

So, is Sub-prime Lending a Bad Thing?

Not at all. In fact, it is often very helpful for those who want to establish credit, or those who are trying to get back on their feet after some rough times. Once a person begins to establish a consistent and positive credit history, then they can move into the prime-lending category.

There are, however, some lenders who take advantage of those who have little knowledge of financial matters, as well as those who have had trouble in the past. This is known as predatory lending and should not be confused with sub-prime lending. For more information on sub-prime vs. predatory lending, see Appendix B.

What Can I Do to Get the Prime Rate?

The best thing you can do is to educate yourself on your finances. The following are also some simple tips to improve your credit score and your opportunity for financial independence:

- Eliminate delinquent payments—Pay bills on time and as agreed, and also avoid filing for bankruptcy unless there is absolutely, positively no other option.
- Avoid frequent credit applications—Inquiries themselves can lower your score, so try not to apply for every credit card offer you receive in the mail.
- Reduce credit-card balances—Scores are lowered if all of your cards are maxed out, so do your best to keep them under their limit.

- Eliminate credit card balances—The best way to do this is to pay more than just the minimum monthly payment. And if you have more than one card, start on the lowest one, and just keep working on it until they are all done. It will take time but can be done.
- Avoid borrowing from companies that do not report your positive history to credit bureaus—Some companies only report the negative, so ask your lender if they report your information to one or more of the credit bureaus. .
- Review your credit report(s) annually and correct all errors— Knowing what is on your credit report is key. Make sure all of the information is correct, and take the steps needed to remove incorrect information.
- Take financial education classes—Knowing the terms of lending and how to read a credit report can help you break the debt cycle and improve your score.
- Use electronic payment systems when available—Doing so helps to avoid missed payments due to unexpected deployments or extended training.
- Consider using specialty financial services companies—There are companies that do not have FICO limits and do not have rank restrictions.
- Use a reputable company—Check companies that have been around for a long time, employ certified counselors, and have a history of offering financial education.

In conclusion, no matter what model or scores are used, the military families with the best money management habits will have a better chance of getting credit and will do so at a lower cost. Even if you are a sub-prime borrower right now, you can earn your way into the prime category.

Appendix B

Sub-prime Loans for Military Families: Valuable or Predatory?

What is "Sub-prime" Lending?

Sub-prime lending is simply offering loans or other types of credit that have higher interest rates than a "prime" rate. This type of lending provides access to credit for consumers who are unable to qualify for this "prime" rate because of a poor or limited credit history, and is important because it allows those who have less-than-perfect credit have access to loans. Military personnel—particularly younger service members—frequently access this type of lending.

With this type of lending comes a higher amount of risk for the company or institution making the loan or offering the credit. Most regulators and consumer groups do not object to true risk-based pricing; they simply want to ensure adequate safeguards to prevent lenders from taking advantage of borrowers.

What is "Predatory" Lending?

Predatory lending can be defined as that which takes advantage of borrowers by charging excessive fees or using deliberate deception to hide the questionable nature of the transaction. Predatory lending practices often involve very high interest rates, lack any consideration of the borrower's ability to repay and typically allow unrestricted rollovers.

Customers who fall victim to such practices quickly find themselves in a seemingly endless cycle of debt. In the past few years, the subject of predatory lending has become more visible than ever and usually refers to

157

easy-to-get loans that are intentionally structured to be deceptive and disadvantageous to borrowers.

Predatory lending can include payday lending, title pawn lending, bank overdraft fees, credit cards that rely on minimum monthly payments, or even mortgage lending. Consumers who are most likely a target of these practices are frequently sub-prime borrowers. Common belief says that predatory lending is an "outside the gate" issue created by small or unscrupulous lenders. These practices, however, also occur in big banks and credit unions, including some that are operating on military installations.

So Are All Sub-prime Lenders Predatory?

No. In fact, growth in the sub-prime market over the past several years is beneficial and a valuable service to many people, including military families. Certain people will have a low credit score for a number of reasons: frequent moves, low income, poor credit, or simply insufficient credit history due to age, are a number of reasons for a low credit score. Sub-prime lending is called such because of the risk—in other words, if a company is a sub-prime lender, they often work with people who have lower credit scores and are a higher risk for a loan or other line of credit. These sub-prime lenders charge a higher Annual Percentage Rate (or "APR") than conventional lenders due to the higher risk.

It is when lenders take unfair advantage of customers that the lending becomes predatory. This can include a number of practices, such as allowing customers to take out additional loans to pay for their previous loans (known as "flipping"), not truly sharing the interest rate and APR with the customer (instead, the company just says it's a flat fee per dollar amount), or not truly determining whether or not their customers can pay off the debt.

In a letter to the United States Treasury Department's Office of Thrift Supervision, Curtis L. Page, chairman and president of Home Federal Bank, writes, "There is a significant distinction between predatory lending and sub-prime lending. Predatory lending is a pricing strategy and sub-prime lending is a credit underwriting evaluation."[1]

What is Being Done to Stop Predatory Lending?

The Federal Reserve Board has responded to the increase in predatory lenders with new guidelines that will go into effect in October of 2004. The Fed will also prevent loan "flipping" and will require that lenders document that the borrower has the ability to repay the loan before giving one to a consumer.

In addition to these measures, the Fed has also renewed the study of bank and credit union programs that are sometimes called "bounce protection," "courtesy protection" or "overdraft privilege." These services are promoted as ways to cover a bad check for a certain amount of time. But the high fees of $20 and up are disguised loans because banks are, in reality, charging interest rates of 240 percent or more.

Many states are also examining solutions, most related to either full disclosure or APR limits for certain transactions. It is clear that their focus is on predatory lending practices only—every effort is being made not to curtail sub-prime borrowing opportunities to those who might not otherwise qualify for loans.

What Can I Do to Protect Myself From Predatory Lenders?

When you borrow money, make sure to ask for all information, because sometimes what looks like a good deal may in fact be a bad one.

- Ask for full disclosure—a sub-prime lender will tell you up-front about the interest rate and APR, as well as any fees associated with your loan. A predatory lender most often will not.
- Make sure the company calculates your debt ratio—if they don't, they are not checking to see if you can truly re-pay the loan.

---

1 Curtis L. Hage, in a letter to the Office of Thrift Supervision, http://www.ots.treas.gov/docs/9/96673.pdf

- Make sure the company reviews your credit report to ensure your ability to repay the debt.
- Make sure the company will supply the credit bureau with information about this loan—your best chance to improve your credit score is to prove you can pay your obligation on time and in full.

In summary, those institutions that offer specific, sub-prime lending options perform a needed service and are not necessarily predatory. There is a very clear line between predatory and sub-prime lending, and it is important to be clear about what distinguishes responsible, risk-based pricing from predatory lending. When someone has to borrow money, they should ask all of the right questions, insist on full disclosure, and know the true costs and terms to ensure that they are making an informed decision.

Printed in the United States
22121LVS00004BB/85-510